Revolution
of the Word

JEROME ROTHENBERG

Tching prayed on the mountain and
                wrote MAKE IT NEW
on his bath tub
                Day by day make it new
cut underbrush
pile the logs
keep it growing.
—EZRA POUND, *Canto 53*

REVOLUTION
OF THE

WORD

*A New Gathering of American
Avant Garde Poetry 1914-1945*

A CONTINUUM BOOK
THE SEABURY PRESS · NEW YORK

for Paul Blackburn

The Seabury Press
815 Second Avenue
New York, N. Y. 10017
Copyright ©1974 by Jerome Rothenberg
Designed by Judith Lerner
Printed in the United States of America

Library of Congress Cataloging in Publication Data

Rothenberg, Jerome, 1931–
    Revolution of the word; a new gathering of American
avant garde poetry, 1914–1945.

    (A Continuum book)
    1. American poetry—20th century. I. Title.
PS615.R67   811'.5'208   73–17883
ISBN 0–8164–9205–0

Grateful acknowledgment is made to the following for permission to use material:

The Francis Bacon Foundation, Inc. for works by Walter Conrad Arensberg: "Dada Is American," "Ing," "Vacuum Tires: A Formula for the Digestion of Figments," "Arithmetical Progression of the Verb 'To Be,'" "For 'Shady Hill,' Cambridge, Mass."

Corinth Books for works by Bob Brown: "Eyes," "without any whirr or sputter" from *1450/1950* published by Corinth Books, Inc. Carlton Brown for "The Aquarium Keeper" by Bob Brown.

Harcourt Brace Jovanovich, Inc. for works by E. E. Cummings: "No Thanks, No. 13" copyright, 1935 by E. E. Cummings; renewed 1963, by Marion Morehouse Cummings; "Memorabilia" copyright 1926 by Horace Liveright; renewed, 1954 by E. E. Cummings. Both reprinted from *Complete Poems 1913-1962* by permissions of Harcourt Brace Jovanovich, Inc.

New Directions Publishing Corporation for "The Walls Do Not Fall" by H. D. (Hilda Doolittle); from *H. D. Trilogy*, copyright 1944 by Oxford University Press, © 1972 by Norman Holmes Pearson. Reprinted by permission of New Directions Publishing Corporation.

George Heard Hamilton, translator for "The Bride Stripped Bare by her Bachelors, Even" from *The Green Box* by Marcel Duchamp. Mme. Marcel Duchamp for works by Marcel Duchamp: "Speculations," "SurSENsure," "Men Before the Mirror," "From Rrose Selavy," "Rotative Demi-Sphere with Pun." The Philadelphia Museum of Art: The Louise and Walter Arensberg Collection for "The" by Marcel Duchamp.

Harcourt Brace Jovanovich for material from "Little Gidding" in *Four Quartets* by T. S. Eliot, copyright 1942, 1943 by T. S. Eliot; renewed, 1970 by Esme Valerie Eliot. Reprinted by permission of Harcourt Brace Jovanovich, Inc.

The Estate of Margaret Anderson for works by Else von Freytag-Loringhoven: "Affectionate," "Holy Skirts," "Mineself—Minesoul—and—Mine—Cast-Iron Lover."

Norma G. Berger for works by Marsden Hartley: "Local Boys and Girls Small Town Stuff," "In Confidence with those well—," "Yours with Devotion," "Mediocrity."

Mrs. Herbert Bayer for works by Mina Loy: "Love Songs," "Costa Magic," "Anglo-Mongrels and the Rose."

Macmillan Publishing Company for "An Octopus" by Marianne Moore. Reprinted with permission of Macmillan Publishing Co., Inc. from *Collected Poems*, by Marianne Moore. Copyright 1935 by Marianne Moore, renewed 1963 by Marianne Moore and T. S. Eliot.

New Directions Publishing Corporation for works by Ezra Pound: "Canto XXXIX," and "Canto LIII." Ezra Pound, *The Cantos*. Copyright 1934, 1940 by Ezra Pound, "The Game of Chess." Ezra Pound, *Personae*. Copyright 1926 by Ezra Pound. Reprinted by Permission of New Directions Publishing Corporation. "Vortex". Ezra Pound, first published in *Blast, I*. All rights reserved. Reprinted by permission of New Directions Publishing Corporation, Agents for the Estate of Ezra Pound.

Harcourt Brace Jovanovich for "The People, Yes (section 53) by Carl Sandburg. From *The People, Yes* by Carl Sandburg, copyright 1936 by Harcourt Brace Jovanovich, Inc.; renewed, 1964 by Carl Sandburg. Reprinted by permission of the publishers.

Yale University Press for "They May Be Said To Be Ready" by Gertrude Stein. Reprinted by permission of Yale University Press from *Stanzas in Meditation*, copyright © 1956 by Alice B. Toklas. Random House, Inc. for excerpts from *Lectures in America* by Gertrude Stein. Copyright 1935 and renewed 1963 by Alice B. Toklas. Reprinted by permission of Random House, Inc. Something Else Press for "A Curtain Raiser" by Gertrude Stein. Reprinted by permission of Something Else Press, Inc. The estate and heirs of Gertrude Stein for the following works by Gertrude Stein: "Before the Flowers of Friendship Faded," from *Tender Buttons*, and from *Mother of Us All*.

Random House for "Connoisseur of Chaos" by Wallace Stevens. Copyright 1942 and renewed 1970 by Holly Stevens. Reprinted from *The Collected Poems of Wallace Stevens*, by permission of Alfred A. Knopf, Inc.

New Directions Publishing Corporation for from *Spring & All*. William Carlos Williams, *Imaginations*. Copyright 1923, 1951 by William Carlos Williams, © 1970 by Florence Williams. Reprinted by permission of New Directions Publishing Corporation.

Liveright Publishing Corporation for "The Mango Tree" from *The Collected Poems and Selected Letters and Prose of Hart Crane* by Hart Crane. Permission of Liveright, Publishing, New York. Copyright © 1933, 1958, 1966 by Liveright Publishing Corporation.

Estate of Caresse Crosby, Harry T. Moore, Literary executor for works by Harry Crosby: "Photoheilograph," "Short Introduction to the Word," "Tattoo," "Pharmacie du Soleil," "Academy of Stimulants," "Madman," "I Climb Alone," "Fragment of an Etude for a Sun-Dial," "The Ten Commandments."

Robert Duncan for "An African Elegy" from *The Years As Catches*, Copyright © 1966 by Robert Duncan.

Indiana University Press for "American Rhapsody (2)" and "Agent No. 174 Resigns" from *New and Selected Poems* by Kenneth Fearing, Indiana University Press, 1956. Harcourt Brace Jovanovich for "End of the Seers' Convention" from *Afternoon of a Pawnbroker and Other Poems*, copyright 1943, by Kenneth Fearing; renewed 1971 by Bruce Fearing. Reprinted by permission of Harcourt Brace Jovanovich, Inc.

Black Sparrow Press for "Flag of Ecstasy" copyright © 1972 by Charles Henri Ford. Reprinted from *Flag of Ecstasy* published by Black Sparrow Press.

Carlton Brown for "Readie-Soundpiece" by Abraham Lincoln Gillespie.

Mme. Marie Jolas "Sleep in Ur," "Rimbaud and the Chauffeur," and "Mountain Words" from *I Have Seen Monsters and Angels* (Transition Press, 1938);

(*Acknowledgments continued on page* 260)

Contents

Nothing changes from generation to generation
except the thing seen
and that makes a composition.
—G. STEIN

Pre-face

I AUTOBIOGRAPHY

It was 1948 & by year's end I was seventeen. I had been coming into poetry for two years. My head was filled with Stein & Cummings, later with Williams, Pound, the French Surrealists, the Dada poets who made "pure sound" three decades earlier. Blues. American Indian things from Densmore. Cathay. Bible, Shakespeare, Whitman. Jewish liturgies. Dali & Lorca were ferocious possibilities. Joyce was incredible to any of our first sightings of his work. The thing was to get off on it, to hear one's mind, learn one's own voice. But the message clear & simple was to move. To change. To create one's self & thus one's poetry. A process.

But all that was from the vantage of where I had grown up, a little behind the times, in the Bronx of depression & World War II. To us the news hadn't yet filtered that the age of the modern, the experimental & visionary (for we sensed it even then as vision), had passed: to be replaced by a return to the old forms, to conventional metrics, diction, a responsible modernism, liberal & reformist, rational & refined, & goodbye to the madmen of language. Those were the first lessons of college days. They called it Auden or Lowell, Tate or Wilbur. Middle-ground, like the politics then emerging. It became a question of amelioration. A shift of stance. A little toughening of Tennyson. Change the topic, the conversation. Change the footnotes. Kierkegaard instead of Darwin. Church instead of Nature. But the body of the poem must stay untouched. A virgin. The words must stay untouched. The images must be inherited & the inheritance must be along the line of what was called the "great tradition." Western. Christian. White.

I am trying to reconstruct, too sketchily, a sense of how all of that impinged: & how, because it impinged so much, it was possible, inevitable, that one saw the transformation of modernism into the void of the "new critics" as the way (*the* way) it actually had happened. A few years later, poets of my generation would again break through, but rarely would we challenge the notion that there had been a virtual break in the continuity of avant garde concerns. Rarely would we insist enough that the development of our own traditions had gone on uninterruptedly from their first eruption circa 1914 to their second in the 1950s. And if we said it, pointed out the irrelevance of the academic middle-grounders or resurrected the work of a (token) handful of survivors, the histories & anthologies were slower to respond & tell our story.

So I must sketch the other account first, the way it continues to be told among the academics: then give a sense of how we found our way to new views of our own immediate pre-history, & what aspects of those views this anthology is trying to present. For we are all, in different ways & from our individual perspectives, talking about a virtual revolution in consciousness, & if we can't remember how we got here, we may be talked into denying where we want to go.

II THE WAY WE LEARNED OUR HISTORY

1945–1950. World War II was over, & American poetry (what was then visible of the iceberg) had entered a strange condition. Something called "modern" was taken as an established fact, but so described as to presume a built-in self-destruct system that was already operative in the work of the inheritors. Wrote one of them, Delmore Schwartz: ". . . the poetic revolution, the revolution in poetic taste which was inspired by the criticism of T. S. Eliot . . . has established itself in power." And he gave as an example of new poets writing in "a style which takes as its starting point the poetic idiom and literary taste of the generation of Pound and Eliot," the following from W. D. Snodgrass:

The green catalpa tree has turned
All white; the cherry blooms once more.

In one whole year I haven't learned
A blessed thing they pay you for

—at which David Antin looks back & comments (1972): "The comparison of this updated version of *A Shropshire Lad* . . . and the poetry of the *Cantos* or *The Waste Land* seems so aberrant as to verge on the pathological."

Yet it was typical. Inevitable in fact for those who couldn't distinguish between "the poetic revolution" & a "revolution in taste," or who still thought of taste as an issue. Even an attempt at such distinctions was then unlikely, for the careers of the inheritors were too often literary, resting like the idea of literature itself on a fixed notion of poetry & poem, which might be improved upon but never questioned *at the root*. And behind it too there was a strange fear of "freedom" as that had been articulated by earlier moderns—whether as "free verse" or "free love" or the abandonment of judgment as a bind on the intelligence or of taste as a determinant of value. So if the taste & judgment they still clung to (& which made them critics "inspired by the criticism of T. S. Eliot") demanded "modern" as an article of 20th century faith, they retained it; but they pulled back into traditional & institutional securities, "picking up again the meters" (Schwartz) as a moral buttress against their own despair. And this itself, qua ideology, was seen as part of a *modern* dilemma, which came to define their modern-ism, not as the promise of a new consciousness but as a glorified "failure of nerve."

Something of that sort must have been in Williams' mind when he spoke of *The Waste Land* as the "great disaster to our letters"— the one poetic event strong enough to draw numbers of the young back to the academic & conventional & to slow the momentum of the 1920s' avant garde. The pull-back, anyway, was explicit in Eliot's criticism & the late Tudor verse style of his shorter poems. But it was lurking as well in Pound's & Williams' own discomfort over *free* verse ("the magnificent failure of Walt Whitman"—W. C. W.) & in the need of many in their generation (almost an American obsession) to lay claim to Old World & "anglo-saxon" culture. In the 1920s it appeared in the high rhetoric of Hart Crane's verse—& in his sense that "the rebellion against . . . the so-called classical strictures" had ended—& it spawned the Southern Fugitives ("the only literary movement to begin in a frat house"—K. Rexroth), who pulled the verse back even further, while developing the concept of the new poet-critic.

If that was the line of descent that Schwartz found "taken for granted not only in poetry & the criticism of poetry, but in the teaching of literature" (1958), it's still worth giving in some detail because it has remained the going view of "modern" American poetry between the two world wars. Any such view has to be selective in its construction of the past. Those like Schwartz's begin, typically, by reducing the number of poets whose immediate concern, circa 1914, was, in Williams' words, "the poetic line, the way the image was to lie on the page." Of these, Williams himself, because his verse line remained "open," fared relatively poorly—though never a complete wipe-out like others of whom I'll be speaking later on. Pound managed better but with the stress on the "classicist," fussier side of his early poetics, & Eliot (along with British poets like Yeats) did extremely well. There was also a tendency to include as "modern" a number of conventional or moderately reformist poets like Robinson or Frost—many of whom were more suitable models for the middle-grounders. Among earlier American poets, Dickinson, Poe or Lanier were nearly always possible; Whitman hardly ever.

The idea was, understandably, to lay a reasonable groundwork for the poetry of the inheritors. In the 1920s these included poets like Tate & Ransom (with Hart Crane—praised for his "failure"— somewhere in the wings) or a somewhat younger British poet like Auden, whose metrics & intellectual banter were crucial to the middle-ground of American poetry in the 30s & 40s. (For others, Yvor Winters, who broke from a radical position in the 1920s to a beleaguered traditionalism later on, served a similar role.) In the 30s & 40s poets like Schwartz & Roethke took up similar terrain, joined by such as Lowell, Wilbur & Jarrell, each of considerable importance at the apex of Schwartz's "revolution in poetic taste" & through its decline since then. At the point of the Hall-Pack-Simpson *Anthology of New American & British Poets* (1957), the "revolution" had nearly come full circle (like tastes in furniture, etc.) to a genuine Victorian revival.

III COUNTER-POETICS

While all of this was going on, a series of avant garde emergences was throwing the middle-ground strategy into doubt. The new groupings appearing in the mid-50s (Black Mountain, Beats, the New York school, deep image, concrete poetry, chance processes, etc.) re-explored the idea of an avant garde, with nearly complete indifference to academic strictures. Poetry was transformative, not only of its present & future, but of its past as well. Primitive & archaic, esoteric & subterranean, non-western & foreign, each had a part to play in a greater "great tradition." Wrote Gary Snyder: "We are witnessing a surfacing (in a specifically 'American' incarnation) of the Great Subculture which goes back as far perhaps as the late Paleolithic."

In that charged atmosphere, the immediate past (but specifically the idea of "poetic revolution") was also undergoing changes. Charles Olson presented his "projective verse" as a synthesis of experiments by "Cummings, Pound, Williams" & pointed to the "objectivists" of the early 1930s as crucial to the process. New magazines like *Black Mountain Review* & *Origin* began to attend to poets like Rexroth & Zukofsky, while Jonathan Williams' Jargon Press was systematically restoring work by Lowenfels, Zukofsky, Patchen, Mina Loy, Bob Brown, etc. Elsewhere James Schuyler, speaking for himself & poets like Frank O'Hara, wrote: "Duchamp's . . . Rrose Sélavy has more to do with poetry written by the poets that I know than that Empress of Tapioca, the White Goddess." And Duchamp was also a force behind the chance poetry & music of such as John Cage & Jackson Mac Low—along with Gertrude Stein, whose presence (ignored by the quasi-"Moderns") was of pivotal importance for poets from Robert Duncan to David Antin to Ted Berrigan to, needless to say, the present editor. Or ranging further, Allen Ginsberg left no doubt about his generation's relation to Whitman & Blake, as well as continuities from despised free verse traditions, rhythm & blues, & the ideological & behavioral implications of Surrealism as mediated by American magazines like *Transition, View* & *VVV*. Other ties to the European & Latin-American avant gardes were at the heart of "deep image" theory & practice, while concrete poetry was a development from European poets like Apollinaire & the Dutch *De Stijl* movement, along with Americans as well known as E. E. Cummings or as submerged as Harry Crosby.

With all that in mind, the progress of American poetry takes on a very different shape—not just a change of names or personnel but a counterpoetics that presents (if I can bring it all together by a great simplification) a fundamentally new view of the relationship between consciousness, language & poetic structure: what is seen, said & made. In the working out of that relationship, lies the great strength of modern poetry as I understand it. And because the line of the New Critics, etc., failed to confront it meaningfully, their work (though it remains the "official" account of the period) seems to me a backwash rather than a living center.

The turning point, anyway, is just before & during World War I, & the range of poets whose work applies is considerable, highly individualized, & very difficult to pin down. But from where I am at present, I'll try to outline some of the questions & propositions I find of interest then & now & (crucial to the story of this book) in the time between:

(1) There is a widespread feeling circa 1914 that consciousness (man's awareness of himself in time & space) is changing. This is taken as both a crisis & an opportunity, & presupposes a continuous need to confront & to integrate new experience & information. A common explanation connects this change, alteration or expansion of consciousness with technological change (the basic condition of the *modern* world) or, more specifically, with a revolution in communications & an easing of cultural & psychic boundaries that together produce an "assault" of alternative ideas & forms. In a world in which "so much happens and anybody at any moment knows everything that is happening," Gertrude Stein sees the artist as the person who "inevitably has to do what is really exciting." And when Pound writes (1915) of a basic poetic process that involves "a rush of experience into the vortex" (i.e., the mind), he is talking about a condition that has become newly critical.

(2) In terms of his immediate experience, the modern poet often shares with his ancient prototype, the shaman, a fundamental concern

with the thing seen.* He is himself the one who sees & projects his vision to others. The individuality of his vision, & the stress he puts on it, may vary, & he may speak of in-sight or of objectification: the intensification of ego or its suppression. No poet solves the problem of vision under these changed circumstances, & by our own time, it becomes evident that the function of poetry isn't to impose a single vision or consciousness but to liberate similar processes in others. The point, which will come up again & again in this anthology, is that the concern with "seeing" is at the heart of the enterprise: e.g., Pound's "image" as the "primary pigment of poetry"; Stein's change of the thing seen as the key to composition; Crane's "poetic prophecy" qua "perception"; Oppen's faith that "the virtue of the mind is that emotion which causes to see"; even Duchamp's "shop window proof of the existence of the exterior world," etc.

(3) When the poet confronts still different kinds of knowing, sees himself with others in time, the "rush of experience" opens into history. In American poetry, this concern stands prominent. But where the ideas truly "rush," the process no longer links event to event in good straight lines, but in the face of multiple chronologies, many poets turn to synchronicity (the simultaneous existence of all places & times) as a basic organizing principle. As a method, a process of making the poem, this becomes "collage": not history but "the dramatic juxtaposition of disparate materials without commitment to explicit syntactical relations between elements" (D. Antin). It is through synchronicity & collage—not only applied to the past but to local & personal particulars—that the modern poem is open to everything; that it becomes the vehicle for "anything the mind can think."

(4) As the "poetic domain" expands to include the possibility of all human experience, a medium is needed flexible enough to get it said. To project the rush of disparate ideas & images (both a lot & a little), poets turn to every means afforded by language: "all words that exist in use" (Whitman), all levels & styles of language,

---

* I have made this comparison, starting from the shaman's side, in **Technicians of the Sacred** (1968), & would suggest the reader check it out there & in **Shaking the Pumpkin** (1972) & **America a Prophecy** (1974). The point of a coincidence between "primitive" & "modern" remains important, though unnecessary to pursue it here.

borrowings from other languages, new words or word distortions (punnings), visual signs, experiments with animal & mediumistic language, even clichés & old poeticisms where the content demands it. Metrics give way to measure—"not the sequence of the metronome" (Pound) but a variable succession of sounds & silences, breath- or mind-directed, a "musical line" derived from the complex movements of actual speech. The written text becomes the poem's notation or, in the formulation of visual & concrete poets, a space in which the eye reads visible shape & meaning at a single glance. Here & there too, one sees the first experiments with performance & a fusion with the other arts—towards "intermedia" & the freedom of a poetry without fixed limits, which may change at any point into something else.

(5) With such means at his disposal, the poet can enter on a career as a prophet & revolutionary, a cultist or a populist by turns. Or he can, in a more profound sense, become the person who keeps raising alternative propositions, eluding the trap of his own visions as he goes.

IV   CHRONOLOGY

The idea of a poetry that was revolutionary in structure & word was carried by an "advance guard" (several in fact) from early in the century until the new poetic revolution of the 1950s. In turn these first avant garde poets had received it, qua prophecy, from poets & artists just before them, as well as from a range of older poetries, subterranean traditions that were being uncovered piecemeal & read as alternative views of poetic origins & the "nature of the real." The roots were set, & by 1913 the new shoots were appearing at the surface.

That year, 1913, is the key to the initial groupings in the present book. Three germinal events to be noted—of which only one, "imagism(e)," is still given sufficient attention in the histories of poetry. A playful move by Pound, as British correspondent for *Poetry*, to provide a "movement" (complete with frenchified name) for his work, H. D.'s & Richard Aldington's, it offered a series of principles ("do's & don't's") as a "classicist" interpretation of the free verse practiced by earlier American followers of Whitman. But almost immediately it split into the "imagism" of Amy Lowell & others (an amalgam of free verse & haiku, etc.) & Pound's own development of "vorticist" theory over the next several years. Typically enough, it's "imagism" that retains a place in the literary histories, while the vorticist proposals, crucial to one aspect of collage in U.S. poetry, are inevitably left to the "Poundians."

The two other "events" of 1913 were the Armory art show in New York & the appearance, prior to the publication the following year of *Tender Buttons*, of some of Gertrude Stein's writings in a special number of Stieglitz's magazine, *Camera Work*. The Armory Show didn't just introduce European art (cubism, futurism, etc.) to America, but, as witnessed by Williams & others, it "brought to a head" the "great surge of interest in the arts generally" that was "seething" in places like New York & Chicago before World War I. In that context Stein's work appeared as a cubist poetry that went beyond French poets like Apollinaire, offering strategies of composition & language that remain at the limits of modern poetry sixty years later.

This interplay of poetry & art has been viewed with suspicion by those for whom poetry exists in a basically literary framework. Yet it was crucial, & many poets besides Williams & Stein have testified to its importance. After the start of World War I, Pound joined the British novelist & cubist painter, Wyndham Lewis, in preparation of *Blast*, a polemical, Futurist-styled magazine that turned "imagism" into vorticism & set much of the groundwork for Pound's own *Cantos*. In America, *Camera Work* & its successor, *291*, provided a place for both artists & poets, publishing work by Stein & Apollinaire, early writings by the painter-poet, Marsden Hartley, & Mina Loy's "Aphorisms on Futurism" (1914), which introduced her as another germinal & now astonishingly neglected poet. And in 1915, Marcel Duchamp came to New York, to settle in the U.S. & contribute work as both an artist (or anti-artist) & a poet writing in French, English & a visual/mental language somewhere beyond both.

The Duchamp nexus is also overlooked & crucial. With Picabia, Man Ray & Walter Conrad Arensberg, Duchamp heated up the general American climate & provided a link between the Zurich Dadaists of 1917 & the American version that preceded them. The local Dada work appeared in several magazines edited by Duchamp & Arensberg, & shared space in *Rogue* & Alfred Kreymborg's *Others*. While nohow as homogeneous as a short summary might make it sound, the "movement" (when supplemented by the wider context provided by Kreymborg & the Others group) included poets like Bob Brown, Mina Loy, Else von Freytag-Loringhoven, Maxwell Bodenheim, & Marsden Hartley, along with Williams, who was a link in turn to the Pound-Eliot nexus developing in Britain. And in Chicago, *The Little Review* (edited by Margaret Anderson & Jane Heap) provided similar juxtapositions of the new poetry, by following a year of Pound's guest editorship that focused on himself, Eliot, Joyce, Yeats, & Lewis, with a heavy concentration on poets like Freytag-Loringhoven, Loy & Stein, installments of Joyce's *Ulysses*, & an attempt through the early 20s to keep the European avant garde at the center of American attentions.

During that first post-war decade, many of the early poets remained central to the new developments—or, like Williams, increased their range & influence. Still others like Stevens & Cummings took independent positions that covered additional areas of structure & vision. And the first "disappearances" began: Duchamp's exaggerated withdrawal from art (while the writings as Rrose Sélavy went on in French), Else von Freytag-Loringhoven's return to Europe & a tragic death, & the increasing silence of Mina Loy after her long poem, "Anglo-Mongrels & the Rose," appeared in installments in *The Little Review* & Robert McAlmon's *Contact*.

The Surrealists had by then begun to move in European poetry & art, & the influence though not the institution spread to America as well. Outside France, the political & social sides of the movement weakened considerably, while its psychic aspects (the incorporation of dream into everyday life, etc.) had a variety of effects, from thickening the avant garde plot & helping to trigger the later psychedelic revolution, to becoming a kind of fashionable window dressing, devoid of its initial freedom & terror. Nor was it only the Surrealists who carried the message. Eliot's *Waste Land*, when it appeared, wasn't the simple "disaster" described by Williams, but coincided with the haunted world of Surrealism, where:

. . . bats with baby faces in the violet light
Whistled, and beat their wings
And crawled head downward down a blackened wall
And upside down in air were towers . . .

And it was also the first American poem on deliberate collage principles to surface & exert an influence on modern poetry throughout the world.

The "crisis in consciousness" (Mina Loy, 1914) had become overt. Questions of "vision" & the "thing seen" (or dreamed, etc.) began to dominate avant garde poetry, often to the neglect of parallel questions of "structure" & "language." Hart Crane, for example, used a form of collage construction as a means for "prophecy" but drew back from any serious reconstitution of the verse line, opting finally for a return to the older "poetic" language. Thus he stands between poets like Allen Tate on his "right" & Harry Crosby on his "left," with both of whom he had significant contacts. Crosby, whose Black Sun Press in Paris first published Crane's *The Bridge*, was a poet whose mythic obsessions (sun gods & goddesses, etc.) surfaced in a variety of new forms: prose poems, long verse incantations, & early concrete & found poetry. He shares a position, strongly influenced by the Surrealists & early vision/structure experimenters like Blake, Rimbaud & Lautreamont, with Eugene Jolas & even younger poets like Charles Henri Ford & Parker Tyler. Jolas' *Transition* (slogan: "the revolution of the word") brought together Surrealist "dream-time" with extensions, by such as Joyce, Stein & the nearly forgotten Abraham Lincoln Gillespie, of what Pound called *logopoeia* ("a dance of the intelligence among words . . .")—though obviously beyond Pound's tolerance for same.

Elsewhere many poets, responding to the intensifying politics of the 20s & 30s, found the open verse line, related use of speech rhythms, & incorporative techniques like collage, viable instruments for a new public & political poetry. If the anthologies & histories give the impression that modern American poetry was dominated by poets far to the right of their European counterparts, it's partly because they represent the work of the 20s & 30s by poets who were conservative in most aspects of their lives. Social poetry (so-called) has been too easily disdained by the middle-grounders, although many of the poets sometimes identified with it (Patchen, Lowenfels, Fearing, Rukeyser, etc.) were also important in the development of other avant garde concerns & stances that would serve as models for poets & counter-culturists after World War II.

It's a curious fact too that the younger American poets who developed the structural side of the equation & explored vision as a process of eye & mind ("objectivism") were all at the same time involved in left-wing politics. Zukofsky, Oppen, Reznikoff, & Rakosi are the "objectivists" who have re-emerged over the last twenty years, as the precursors of some of the dominant post-World War II strategies. Allying themselves with Pound & Williams (but note the differences in political stance) they developed unique extensions of imagist & vorticist poetics—toward what Zukofsky called "the direction of historic & contemporary particulars." Zukofsky, who acted as their theoretician & compiler (*An "Objectivists" Anthology*, 1932), was one of the most far-reaching innovators in the whole American side of the modernist enterprise, yet neglected with the others until his rediscovery, circa 1950, by the Black Mountain poets. His career in that way is a little like Kenneth Rexroth's, some of whose long poems from the 20s he published in his anthology & the "Objectivists" issue of *Poetry* (1931). While Rexroth was probably too independent to accept the "Objectivists" association, he had developed an "objective" collage technique of his own, which he identified with "literary cubism" as a "restructuring of experience . . . purposive, not dreamlike . . . an uncanniness fundamentally different in kind from the most haunted utterances of the Surrealist or Symbolist unconscious."

By World War II, the avant garde publishing network (much of it in Europe) had been badly disrupted, & in the hiatus that followed, the universities & a sprinkling of literary "reviews" stood out as the purveyors of a highly attenuated modernism, mediated by the Nashville Critics, etc., whose way was made easier by a growing avant garde inability to reconcile the demands of structure & vision. Some poets like Oppen & Lowenfels had stopped writing; others like Zukofsky had withdrawn; & still others had made a resigned truce with the high-riding new traditionalists. But the presence in New York of Breton & other Surrealist exiles made some difference even then, & a number of magazines & little presses (*View, VVV,* Bern

Porter's publications in California) offered a transitional alliance of poets & artists, basically Surrealist in outlook. So the enterprise continued, marked by new appearances, whose significance would only become clear in the following decade: Robert Duncan as co-editor of *The Experimental Review*; Philip Lamantia as a 15-year-old poet discovered by Breton; Charles Olson, right after the war, as the last American poet published by the Crosbys' Black Sun Press; & others, like Mac Low & Cage, not out in public yet as poets. The lines of transmission were tangled but they were clearly there, & a new generation was already born & waiting to receive & extend them.

V THIS BOOK & MORE

In *America a Prophecy* (1973) George Quasha & I attempted a re-view of the entire range of North American poetry "from pre-Columbian times to the present." In that rush of poems & historical forms, largely arranged achronologically, we were able to signal the existence of poets & modes of poetry within any given period, but not to give a representative view of *all* the poets included or to put enough work back into print to provide a detailed picture of the times in which they worked. So it seemed to me that that book, to be germinal, would have to generate a number of other works—more precise views of the periods in question.

The present anthology is such an attempt—central, for the reasons stated above, to my own sense of the poetic present & past. Its perspective & structure reflect a need to affirm a series of continuities & to provide a useful range of materials in a manageable number of pages. To handle that I've limited the number of poets included, so that individuals & groups (particularly those neglected or suppressed till very recently) could be shown in more than a token way. With moderns like Pound, Cummings or Williams, whose work is easily available, I've kept the page count down, while highlighting aspects that seem to me crucial &/or played-down in more cautious appraisals. And except for a few obvious pieces, I've avoided overlappings with *America a Prophecy*, hoping that the reader will turn there for complementary poems & data & will go beyond both to a review of other gatherings & to the "collected works" (however difficult to obtain) of the poets themselves.

I have divided the book into two sections, in each of which the poets appear in alphabetical order. The first section consists of poets whose work had begun to appear by 1920 (actually from somewhat before World War I to somewhat after), while the second presents a kind of avant garde middle generation, fundamental to the continuity that the book proposes & including a few poets (Olson, Mac Low, Duncan) who will more clearly emerge in the 1950s—where Donald Allen's *New American Poetry* & other anthologies will pick up the story. Because many of the poets are unknown or aren't as well-known as they should be (& because I want to make clear from what perspectives I'm viewing the others), I've provided head-notes for each poet, giving the essential data, dates & publications, with some further comments by myself & others. From time to time too, I've supplemented the obvious anthology selections with documents & brief quotes that may provide an additional, if emblematic, context for the poems. For similar reasons, I've decided to keep some selections in their original typography or in the poet's hand, where that seemed important to the poem or to its position in time & place. Finally, I've tried to resist the anthologizer's temptation to cut big poems into little ones, since it seems to me that the "long poem" itself is a significant development of collage composition.

My intention throughout hasn't so much been to convince some hypothetical, entrenched opponents, of the rightness of my own view of things, as to make a body of material available to those who need it or are looking for the sources of a poetry that has (in its later forms) already changed their lives. I would be more than satisfied if the presentation followed *America a Prophecy* in returning a number of poems & poets to circulation: those like Crosby, Jolas, Gillespie & Freytag-Loringhoven, no gatherings of whose work currently exist; others like Loy, Brown or Hartley, some of whose poetry has been reissued since World War II but is no longer in circulation; still others like Stein & Duchamp, where the personality is well-known, but the impact lessened by their virtual exclusion from anthologies & histories of modern poetry; or, like Zukofsky, Rexroth, Patchen & Oppen, poets who remained active & influential, but whose importance has been played down in favor of their more cautious contemporaries.

Once I chose to present some of these poets in detail, I found that I had consequently to omit a number of others whose work also concerns me & who may have played an even greater role for other of my contemporaries. Since I'm painfully aware of the danger of anthologies, I try to use them for presenting work & initiating discussion, while at the same time avoiding the trap of repression by omission. At least I would make clear that I see anthologies as a device for signalling what's possible in poetry, not as an authoritarian guide to poems or poets. In this spirit I've suggested turning to the poets' "complete works" or, where unavailable, encouraging their return to print. For the poets omitted here, I can only point to the entries (however token) in *America a Prophecy* & offer the following supplementary list of poets, known & unknown, who are in varying degree part of that still larger avant garde anthology I carry in my mind:

WITHIN THE EARLY GENERATION: Conrad Aiken, Sherwood Anderson, Arturo Giovannitti, Robinson Jeffers, Vachel Lindsay (the intermedia work combining poetry with dance, film, hieroglyphics), Edgar Lee Masters, Man Ray.

WITHIN THE MIDDLE GENERATION: Paul Bowles, Kay Boyle, Kenneth Burke, Emanuel Carnevali, Malcolm Cowley, Horace Gregory, Langston Hughes, James Laughlin, Haniel Long, Archibald MacLeish, Robert McAlmon, Lorine Niedecker, Carl Rakosi, M. C. Richards, Theodore Roethke, Muriel Rukeyser, Eli Siegel, Melvin B. Tolson, Parker Tyler, Jose Garcia Villa, John Brooks Wheelright.

POETS WHOSE WORK EMERGES IN THE 50S & BEYOND: John Cage, William Everson, David Ignatow, Philip Lamantia, Bern Porter.

And even here the rundown is incomplete & fails as well to mention the effect on later avant gardes of both oral & blues poets like Lightning Hopkins, John Lee Hooker, Bukka White, & so on, & the great range of modern European poetry that has been an ongoing & crucial presence.

VI ACKNOWLEDGEMENTS

In so far as this gathering is part of the unfinished business of *America a Prophecy*, my primary acknowledgements are to George Quasha, with whom I first searched out many of the poems contained herein & tried to put them in perspective. Any divergences from that configuration are my own responsibility or the result of additional discoveries & experience with the materials at hand. I'm also grateful for the help given by David Antin, who has been a friend & often unacknowledged collaborator for most of my life now, & whose essay, "Modernism & Postmodernism: Approaching the Present in American Poetry" (*Boundary 2*, No. 1, 1972), provided a very useful, polemical summary of the conflict between middle-ground & avant garde modernism in the 40s & 50s. Nor can I let the occasion go by without expressing warm thanks to Jonathan Williams, whose Jargon Books have brought much of the earlier poetry to light for my generation; to James Laughlin, who has promoted the idea of "new directions" in poetry for the last four decades; & to Kenneth Rexroth, who has constantly reminded us, in books like *American Poetry in the 20th Century*, of how much more of an avant garde there has been than the standard anthologies were ever willing to acknowledge. I'm additionally indebted to Rexroth & to Carol Tinker for assistance in initiating the present volume; & I'm mindful that conversations with him, like others last Spring with George & Mary Oppen, helped greatly to sharpen my sense of the condition of poetry in the 20s & 30s.

Finally, Laura Riding, who is probably in opposition to most of the views presented here, was extremely generous in correspondence & in mapping out a selection from her work. I remain deeply appreciative of that work itself & of the ultimate, unswerving & useful questioning of poetry to which she has led us.

Still other advice on specific poets was freely given by Barry Alpert & Allen De Loach, particularly on the work of Pound, Lowenfels, Zukofsky, & Freytag-Loringhoven; & George Butterick helped greatly by clarifying the chronology of Charles Olson's work before 1945. I was also assisted throughout by Karl Gay & the staff

of the Lockwood Library Poetry Collection at the University of
Buffalo, for whose kindness & generosity I will be forever grateful.
In much the same way, Anne D'Harnoncourt of the Philadelphia
Museum of Art gave indispensable help in surveying the work of
Marcel Duchamp & Walter Conrad Arensberg. My editors at Sea-
bury Press were George Lawler, who started the project, & Karen
Ready, who happily advanced it; & in the day to day construction of
the book, my wife, Diane, was my constant reader & adviser.

What is more difficult to acknowledge is the significance for
me of nearly two decades of contact with my contemporaries in
what Paul Blackburn used to think of as the "republic of poets." It
would be pointless to list all those who have taught me by a free
discussion of our mutual aspirations towards a new poetry or a
return to the ever present origins of poetry within the human mind.
I trust they know who they are & that no disagreements & distances
can lessen the gratitude I feel for having lived among them.

JEROME ROTHENBERG
October 1973
Salamanca, New York

ONE

Preliminaries

TODAY is the crisis in consciousness.
—MINA LOY (1914)

Walter Conrad Arensberg

Born 1878 in Pittsburgh. Died 1954. Remembered mostly for the art collections he founded, his home in N.Y.C. was a center during World War I for poets & artists like Duchamp, Picabia, Man Ray, Marsden Hartley, Mina Loy. After 1916 his own poetry turned to radical explorations of language & structure, appearing in magazines like *Rogue*, his own *Blind Man*, Kreymborg's *Others* (which he helped to found), Man Ray's *TNT*, & Picabia's *391*. He moved, from the early 1920s on, to studies of Bacon/Shakespeare, Dante, etc., in search of hidden messages, but his poetry remained a presence in Rexroth's mid-20s "cubism," e.g., & bears an acknowledged resemblance to recent poets like Clark Coolidge & Ron Silliman, who continue to probe the possibility of "abstract" &/or non-syntactical composition. While there's never been a book of Arensberg's "cubist" & Dada poems, some of the earlier work (influenced by French symbolism, etc.) appeared in *Poems* (1914) & *Idols* (1916). What follows may be all the experimental poetry he ever published.

DADA IS AMERICAN

Cubism was born in Spain; France just picked the patent up, didn't even clear it with the state. Too bad, Cubism's a little like French matches, never did catch fire; surface of that box was short on phosphorous. And just when Monsieur Rosenberg's all set to fabricate an enormous box, it turns out that the matches are all soggy, floating around in the mouldy liquid.

Cubism was Spanish, it became Alsacian, now it's dancing on red carpets in a few commercial Paris galleries.

No chance for it to cry: Viva DADA; it's a consumptive on a

chaise-longue; youth has flown out of its mean old eyes; just makes you think of that old lady, Roch Grey; hates her children, speaks of nurses with the utmost scorn.

I've had the urge to say a little about Cubism, being one of those who was expecting something from that geometric word; now I'm forced to admit my disillusionment and at the same time my joy in contemplating DADA, the world-wide representative of everything that's young, alive & playful; Dada whose religion doesn't come out of a cathedral like appendicitis.

DADA is American, DADA is Russian, DADA is Spanish, DADA is Swiss, DADA is German, DADA is French, Belgian, Norwegian, Swedish, Monacan. Anyone who lives without rules, who doesn't love museums except for their floors, is DADA. . . . A true work of Dada shouldn't live more than six hours.

I, Walter Conrad Arensberg, American poet, declare that I am against Dada, seeing no way but that to be up dada, up dada, up dada, up dada.

Bravo, bravo, bravo. Viva Dada.

WALTER CONRAD ARENSBERG

New York   33 West 67 Street

Note. Translated from the French by Jerome Rothenberg.

ING

Ing? Is it possible to mean ing?
Suppose
      for the termination in *g*
               a disoriented
               series
      of the simple fractures
               in sleep.
               Soporific
      has accordingly a value for soap
               so present to
               sew pieces.

                                    And *p* says: Peace is.
And suppose the *i*
                    to be big in ing
                    as Beginning.
                              Then Ing is to ing
as aloud
        accompanied by times
and the meaning is a possibility
                              of ralsis.

VACUUM TIRES: A FORMULA FOR THE DIGESTION OF FIGMENTS

à la la

When the shutter from a dry angle comes between the pin and a special delivery it appears at blue. Likewise in concert with strings on any other flow the clock of third evenings past Broadway is alarming, because it is written in three-four time to chewing gum; if you upset the garter, the r remains west, or to the left of flesh, as in revolving or Rector's. The whole effect is due to blinds, drawn in arithmetic to a sketch of halves, which are smoked into double disks. By such a system of instantaneous tickets a given volume of camera, analyzed for uric acid, leaves a deposit of ten dollars, and the style decrees that human surfaces be worn for transparencies, the price mark being removed from the lapel.

If, however, the showcases are on trolleys, bottles must be corked for the make-up of negroes. Or if a goitre appears in the elevation of the host, a set of false teeth, picked for the high lights by burnt matches, must be arranged at once in three acts. For the first provide electric fixtures that are tuned to cork tips. For the second consideration is flour, thirds being a key that is rarely advertised. Notwithstanding the thermometer into which the conductor spits, the telephone meets in extremes. A window will change the subject for standing room only.

Yet in spite of a Sunday ceiling to the same schedule, condensed into the bucket of a Melba lip-stick, the traffic-cop will empty the ladder to an equal number of rounds. This bandage is the legislature of taxis to taxidermists, hanging the dessert for bricklayers to little remains of cube root. The up town exit may, or may not, be in manuscript, but as a result of the binomial theorem of closing time, the water-mains, whenever they are directed to funerals, will make a vacuum flash.

ARITHMETICAL PROGRESSION OF THE VERB "TO BE"

On a sheet of paper
    dropped with the intention of demolishing
    space
    by the simple subtraction of a necessary plane
draw a line that leaves the present
    in addition
    carrying forward to the uncounted columns
        of the spatial ruin
        now considered as complete
    the remainder of the past.
The act of disappearing
    which in the three-dimensional
    is the fate of the convergent
        vista
is thus
    under the form of the immediate
arrested in a perfect parallel
    of being
    in part.

FOR "SHADY HILL," CAMBRIDGE, MASS.

A drink into home use indicates early Italian. Otherwise
        "the element of how
      keeps insides. Nothing has now."

But after the carpet whose usury can eat thirds?

Blunders are belted in cousins. Use what listens on Sunday, and catchy elms will oxidize pillows. Any need is original in absence.

The clothes are on the parlor. They are acted by buttons. To extract the meet, invert as if to the light, registering the first position at half. The passage is in time.

As at the end of an equation of two to green,

> *which have the butters of extra broken*
> *on badges biting a needle to partners*
> *if only the bridge is fluent*
> *let it not nice.*

INTERFERE IN ORDER TO MORrow was once upon a time-PIECE OF MY MInd you do not

AXIOM

From a determinable horizon

absent

spectacularly from a midnight

which has yet to make public

a midnight

in the first place incompatibly copied

the other

in observance of the necessary end

guarantees

the simultaneous insularity

of a structure

self-contained

a little longer

than the general direction

of goods opposed

tangentically.

THEOREM

For purposes of illusion
   the actual ascent of two waves
     transparent to a basis
     which has a disappearance of its own
is timed
   at the angle of incidence
       to the swing of a suspended
          lens
from which the waves wash
     the protective coloration.
Through the resultant exposure
     to a temporal process
an emotion
   ideally distant
     assumes on the uneven surface
        descending
   as the identity to be demonstrated
the three dimensions
    with which it is incommensurate.

Bob Brown

Born 1886. Died 1959. He began, circa 1914, to write a low key, highly idiomatic poetry, in which "problems" of language & detail were resolved in an unpretentious, playful manner resembling the strategies of younger New York School poets in the 1960s. First experiments with visual poetry ("eyes on the half shell," below) appeared in Duchamp's *The Blind Man* in 1917; later published as *1450/1950* by Harry Crosby's Black Sun Press, reprinted (1959) by Jonathan Williams' Jargon. In 1931 Brown edited *Readies for Bob Brown's Machine*, a volume of experiments (by Stein, Pound, Jolas, Boyle, McAlmon, Williams, C. H. Ford etc.) in the uses of a tachistoscope-like reading machine: "a moving type spectacle . . . run[ning] on forever before the eye without having to be chopped up into columns, pars, etc." (Of these, A. L. Gillespie's "Readie-Soundpiece" is reprinted in the present gathering, & Brown's own "without any whirr or sputter" is a variant on the same form some years later.) Other books by Brown include *Tahiti* (1915), *My Marjonary* (1916), & *Globe-Gliding* (1930).

Without any whirr or sputter writing will be readable at the speed of the day - 1929 - not 1450. ; it will run on forever before the eye without having to be chopped up into columns, pars & etc. ; not risking the wetting of a single finger to turn a clumsy page - on forever in-a-single-line-I-see-1450-invention-movable-type - Gutenberg - Wynkyn - de -Worde - Jimmy -the-Ink-Caxton-though-Chinese-centuries-before - printed - thousand-page-books-on-silk- leaves-furnished-by-local-silk -worms-no-2-leaves-tinted-alike- printing-from-dainty-porcelain - type - same - stuff - that - makes - teacup - and - dreams ―――― Shakespeare-bending-over-a-work-bench-making - my - language - laboriously - like - a - bellowing-blacksmith-and-turning-out-little- grotesqueries - at-the-forge-all-on-his-own-to-keep-up-his-interest-in-the-job ―― Stream - of - lusty - steamy-big-fisted-moulders-of-words - fit-by ――― Rabelais - Ben - Jonson - Dan- Defoe-Sterne-Walt-Whitman -Gert- Stein-James-Joyce ――――― Stephen- Crane's- Black - Riders- Crash-by-hell-bent-for-leather-upper-case-and- LOWER-CASE -together-chanting - valorously-dont-give - a-damn-if-I-do-die-do-die ―― Print-in-action-at-last- moveable-type-at-full-gallop- ―――― Carl- Sandburg-flashes-through-like-a-dare-devil- commaless-Cossack - astride-his-mustang-bronco - vocabulary-leaning-far-out-into-the-night-to - pick - up-carefully-placed-phrases-with-his-flashing-teeth――――― My-self - I - see - as - mother - father-to-a-new-scope-for-all-writers-to-come- rhythmical-writers-to-the-eye ―― eye-writers―――― writing-in-an-endless-line-for-my-reading-machine―――― simple-foolproof-machine-with-printed-tape-like-typewriter-ribbon-running-on-before-readers-eyes- giving-reader-chance-of-his-life-to-see-something -hear-something-feel- something- get-a-mental-bellyful-of-writer-right-before-him-bringing-them-closer-together-now-that-there-is-more-reading-and-writing-going-on-more-moving-reading-and-more-moving-writing.――

THE AQUARIUM KEEPER

I chew tobacco moistly
And keep the aquarium.
My gold fish are goopy eyed
And droopy;
The lady ones wear bridal veils
And float about the drawing room
Languorously toying with their
Gorgeous Japanese fans
(That stupid folks call fins)
Closing and opening them dreamily,
Like soft-eyed Spanish senoritas;
Flirting with me,
Flashing filmy handkerchiefs of crepe
And lace before my fascinated eyes.
Pruning their weeping willow tails
For my praise.

I keep a covey of speckled fish
Like quail
And when they fly up in a flock
Greedily gobbling bubbles at the
Top of their tank
I look sharply about
To make sure no sportsman
Has smuggled in a gun
To take a pot shot at my pets.

Stupid fish I'd rather eat than look at,
But my gay, gorgeous ones
Fill the eye better than the belly.
My velvet ones,
Pattern models for silks
By Paul Poiret.
My fluttery, friendly,
Moving fellows;
Futurist fancies
Cubist conceptions

And Whistlerian butterflies
With peacock tails
Straight from Paradise
That little Japs
Would fly for colorful kites
From moss green river banks
Into the swirling blue sky
As they do in Hiroshige prints.
I laugh at my funny fish,
Poke my finger playfully
At the glass
Where lurk my spunky, grumpy
Spiteful ones.

Fish are human.

I've some that swarm like bees around a queen,
Or cannibals about a missionary.
Silly-headed, bobby ones
Always agitated
Fluttering about
On futile-minded businesses.
Athletic ones that go in for
Swimming.
And a lot as common and bickeringly content
As chirping sparrows.

I never like to pass the ponds
Of my goopy nightmare fish
After dining late.
I take out my key a bit nervously
And slip softly in,
Skirting round the other corridor
Where the ghoul eyed submarine fellows
Blink all night,
I sneak as softly as I may
To bed
Without disturbing the ugly looking imps

Whose orbs glint phosphorescently at me;
Never looking into evil
Bad luck fire opal eyes
Or pausing where ghost fish glide;
Restless souls that haunted hulks
Of sunken ships in former incarnations;
Their flashing eyes shooting looks at me like
Serpent's fangs of flame;
Crafty, greedy watchers
That follow my course all the way to bed
As I pass along the chilly corridor.

In the morning
With a fresh quid in my cheek
I chew tobacco moistly
And pass boldly through my aquarium,
Coaxing modest rock fish from their hiding places,
Watching my finny chameleons
Change color like sixteen year old girls.
I go to say good morning
To my flappy old soft-backed sea turtle
Who looks like a floating strip of wall paper.
I crumble crackers with friendly fingers
For my parrot fish,
And sometimes wish I could throw
A sort that resembles
Sniffling pious hypocrites in pews
To my big moray
Who sits smug in a length of sewer pipe all day,
Looks like a boa constrictor
And eats like a pig.

Oh, I have a taste for fish.
My most intimate ones
Are open-eyed innocents,
Some like buttercups,
Others like petals of Japanese quince bloom.
Sometimes I wonder

Who washes the ears of my pink tinted
Shell lustre dears.
And though I've worked here
Most all my life
I've never found out who keeps the colors
Fresh
On the hand-painted oriental ones
Imported from Malay.

In the lot I've some chic little sets for rings.
When I fall in love with a mermaid
(If I can ever find one on land)
I know a special black opal frisker
I'm going to hang round her neck for a pendant.
But I'll never get married
Till I find a girl with hair of burnished gold
As beautiful as the scales
(Which I call petals)
Of my Bermuda Brilliant.
Teeth with the sheen of a shad.
A look sparkling and iridescent
Like my rainbow fish.
But even if she never comes
I'll keep jogging along content;
Pruning my flower garden of fish,
Looking after their teeth, tails and morals
Like a mother would,
Walking meditatively, watchfully
Through the pleasant paths of my aquarium,
Chewing tobacco moistly
And feeling very much at home.

1916

EYES

EYES

MY GODT

WHAT EYES !

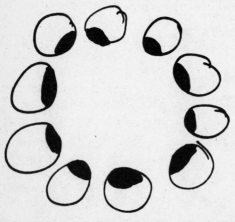

EYES ON THE HALF-SHELL

E.E. Cummings

Born in Cambridge, Mass., 1894. Died 1962. Besides his extensions of conventional forms & themes, Cummings was a major innovator in the use of typography, both as a notational device & as a basis for new visual forms, somewhere along the road to concrete poetry. His insistence on lower-case & innovative punctuation (devices now in common use by poets & others) was a signal that writing, far from being the normative state of a language, is itself derived from speech. While the wide appeal of his modernism has often brought scorn from guardians-of-letters, he has remained a bridge to resources & possibilities for many later poets. Anthology presentation of his work shouldn't obscure the fact that many of his short poems were actually parts of more complicated series & cycles (for which, see comments in Rothenberg/Quasha, *America a Prophecy*). The principal gathering of Cummings' work is *Complete Collected Poems* (1972); earlier books include *Tulips & Chimneys* (1923), *XLI Poems* (1925), *Is 5* (1926), *Viva* (1931), *No Thanks* (1935), *50 Poems* (1940), *1 × 1* (1940), as well as a play, *Him* (1927), & two autobiographical narratives, *The Enormous Room* (1922) & *Eimi* (1933). In his introduction to his own work, below, he reminds us also of the poet as sacred trickster (juggler/jongleur/shaman)—a role forever public.

. . . My theory of technique, if I have one, is very far from original; nor is it complicated. I can express it in fifteen words, by quoting The Eternal Question And Immortal Answer of burlesk, viz. "Would you hit a woman with a child?—No, I'd hit her with a brick." Like

the burlesk comedian, I am abnormally fond of that precision which
creates movement.
1926

NO THANKS, NO. 13
               r-p-o-p-h-e-s-s-a-g-r
         who
a)s w(e loo)k
upnowgath
         PPEGORHRASS
                   eringint(o-
aThe):l
    eA
       !p:
S   a
           (r
rIvInG   .gRrEaPsPhOs)
                      to
rea(be)rran(com)gi(e)ngly
,grasshopper;

MEMORABILIA
stop look &

listen Venezia: incline thine
ear you glassworks
of Murano;
pause
elevator nel
mezzo del cammin' that means half-
way up the Campanile, believe

thou me cocodrillo—

mine eyes have seen
the glory of

the coming of
the Americans particularly the
brand of marriageable nymph which is
armed with large legs rancid
voices Baedekers Mothers and kodaks
—by night upon the Riva Schiavoni or in
the felicitous vicinity of the de l'Europe

Grand and Royal
Danielli their numbers

are like unto the stars of Heaven. . . .

i do signore
affirm that all gondola signore
day below me gondola signore gondola
and above me pass loudly and gondola
rapidly denizens of Omaha Altoona or what
not enthusiastic cohorts from Duluth God only,
gondola knows Cincingondolanati i gondola don't

—the substantial dollarbringing virgins

"from the Loggia where
are we angels by O yes
beautiful we now pass through the look
girls in the style of that's the
foliage what is it didn't Ruskin
says about you got the haven't Marjorie
isn't this wellcurb simply darling"
                                    —O Education:O
thos cook & son

(O to be a metope
now that triglyph's here)

H. D. (Hilda Doolittle)

Born in Bethlehem, Pa. in 1886. Died 1961 in Zurich. In 1912, Pound, as British correspondent for *Poetry*, labelled her an "imagiste" & created a movement largely on the basis of his own work, hers & Richard Aldington's. But her great poems came late in life, beginning with the "war trilogy"—*The Walls Do Not Fall* (1944), *Tribute to the Angels* (1945) & *Flowering of the Rod* (1946)—& ending with *Helen of Egypt* (1961) & the posthumous *Hermetic Definition* (1972), in the course of which the hellenisms of her earlier *Collected Poems* (1925, 1940) opened towards a growing psychic exploration in the light of the oldest Mediterranean mysteries & hermetic traditions. Wrote Robert Duncan: "I see (H. D.'s War Trilogy) develop along lines of an intuited 'reality' that is also a melody of vowel tone and rime giving rise to image and mythos and out of the community of meanings returning to themes towards its individual close. In her work she consciously follows the lead of image to image, of line to line or of word to word, which takes her to the brink . . . of meaning, the poet establishing lines of free (i.e., individual) association within the society of conventional meanings. The form of the poem, of the whole, is on entity of life-time, a 'biological reality,' having life as her own body has life." (*The H. D. Book*, 1961)

From THE WALLS DO NOT FALL

XXXVII

Thou shalt have none other gods but me;
not on the sea

shall we entreat Triton or Dolphin,
not on the land

shall we lift rapt face and clasp hands
before laurel or oak-tree,

not in the sky
shall we invoke separately

Orion or Sirius
or the followers of the Bear,

not in the higher air
of Algorab, Regulus or Deneb

shall we cry
for help—or shall we?

XXXVIII

This search for historical parallels,
research into psychic affinities,

has been done to death before,
will be done again;

no comment can alter spiritual realities
(you say) or again,

what new light can you possibly
throw upon them ?

my mind (yours),
your way of thought (mine),

each has its peculiar intricate map,
threads weave over and under

the jungle-growth
of biological aptitudes,

inherited tendencies,
the intellectual effort

of the whole race,
its tide and ebb;

but my mind (yours)
has its peculiar ego-centric

personal approach
to the eternal realities,

and differs from every other
in minute particulars,

as the vein-paths on any leaf
differ from those of every other leaf

in the forest, as every snow-flake
has its particular star, coral or prism shape.

XXXIX

WE have had too much consecration,
too little affirmation,

too much: but this, this, this
has been proved heretical,

too little: I know, I feel
the meaning that words hide;

they are anagrams, cryptograms,
little boxes, conditioned

to hatch butterflies . . .

XL

FOR example:
Osiris equates O-sir-is or O-Sire-is;

Osiris,
the star Sirius,

relates resurrection myth
and resurrection reality

through the ages;
plasterer, crude mason,

not too well equipped, my thought
would cover deplorable gaps

in time, reveal the regrettable chasm,
bridge that before-and-after schism,

(*before Abraham was I am*)
uncover cankerous growths

in present-day philosophy,
in an endeavour to make ready,

as it were, the patient for the Healer;
correlate faith with faith,

recover the secret of Isis,
which is: there was One

in the beginning, Creator,
Fosterer, Begetter, the Same-forever

in the papyrus-swamp,
in the Judean meadow.

XLI

Sirius :
what mystery is this?

you are seed,
corn near the sand,
enclosed in black-lead,
ploughed land.

Sirius :
what mystery is this?

you are drowned
in the river;
the spring freshets
push open the water-gates.

Sirius :
what mystery is this?

where heat breaks and cracks
the sand-waste,
you are a mist
of snow: white, little flowers.

XLII

O, SIRE, is this the path?
over sedge, over dune-grass,

silently
sledge-runners pass.

O, Sire, is this the waste?
unbelievably,

sand glistens like ice,
cold, cold;

drawn to the temple-gate, O, Sire,
is this union at last?

XLIII

Still the walls do not fall,
I do not know why;

there is zrr-hiss,
lightning in a not-known,

unregistered dimension;
we are powerless,

dust and powder fill our lungs,
our bodies blunder

through doors twisted on hinges,
and the lintels slant

cross-wise;
we walk continually

on thin air
that thickens to a blind fog,

then step swiftly aside,
for even the air

is independable,
thick where it should be fine

and tenuous
where wings separate and open,

and the ether
is heavier than the floor,

and the floor sags
like a ship floundering ;

we know no rule
of procedure,

we are voyagers, discoverers
of the not-known,

the unrecorded ;
we have no map ;

possibly we will reach haven,
heaven.

Marcel Duchamp

Born 1877 in Blainville, France (near Rouen). Died 1968. He came to N. Y. C. in 1915, two years after his "Nude Descending a Staircase" rocked the Armory Show; later became a U. S. citizen, living between Europe & U. S. A. until his death. A major force in the reinvestigation of artistic & poetic categories, he "opened the era of poetic experience in which chance & the concrete thing constitute a poetry that you can pick up in your hand or repulse with a kick" (thus: Georges Hugnet). In America, during World War I, he had an immediate influence on many poets ("strange quickening of artistic life. . . . began to notice that Duchamp was with us"— W. C. W., 1915), helping to create an important (pre)-Dada scene & to forge links with European artists & poets. Edited *New York Dada*, *Rongwrong* & *Blind Man* with such as Arensberg, Picabia & Man Ray. As a progenitor of what would later be known as chance composition, found-poetry &-art (*vide* his "ready-mades," etc.), intermedia, & conceptual art ("to put painting once again at the service of mind"), his work early showed a strong verbal side. Word-play & punning appear both in his titles & in writings under the name Rrose Sélavy (*eros c'est la vie*). While he does give up painting after 1920 (& becomes a chess & proto-Zen master, as the legend goes), he remains an artist & poet, contributes important service to Surrealism, & begins after 1940 to have a new influence on many areas of creativity in U. S. A. His two great erotic works, the early "Large Glass" (The Bride Stripped Bare by Her Bachelors Even) & the posthumously shown "Étant Données" are bridged by the verbal materials & notes which he began to write in 1912 & which came into English in Richard Hamilton's typographical version (1960, under Duchamp's supervision). The principal collection of his writings, including works in English, is *Marchand du Sel* (Paris,

1958), but poems, etc., also appear in *The Complete Works of Marcel Duchamp* (ed. Arturo Schwarz, 1969).

SPECULATIONS
Can one make works which are not works of "art"?

The question of shop windows.˙.
Submit to the interrogation of shop windows.˙.
The insisting of the shop window.˙.
The shop window proof of the existence of the exterior world.˙.
When one submits to the examination of the shop window, one pronounces also one's own sentence. In effect, the choice is "come and go". From the demand of shop windows, from the inevitable response to shop windows, the decision of choice is concluded. No stubbornness, no absurdity,: to hide the coition through a window glass with one or many objects of the shop window. The task consists in breaking the glass and in rueing it as soon as possession is consummated. Q.E.D.   Neuilly   1913

SURcenSURE

                    I wish to state in the first place that
          . . . .
          . . . .
          . . . . that he is the
          first in the world, and notably superi-
          or . . . .
          We approve beforehand . . . .
          . . . . . . which he commands . . .
          . . . .
          we are convinced that . . . .
          . . . . inspired by the highest

motives.

We will therefore voluntari-
ly . . . .

. . . .

. . . . the pity is . . . . .

. . . .

. . . .

Of which he is therefore entirely inno-
cent . . . .

. . . .

. . . . causes
us simultaneous joy and despair . . . . .

. . . .

. . . .

. . . .

compelled as we are to ramble on about
physiognomy . . . .

. . . .

. . . . It was a feat of strength

. . . .

comrades of Phynance, as father Ubu used
to say . . . .

. . . .

. . . .

. . . .

. . . .

. . . .

But take care !

. . . .

. . . .

Note. Translation from French in catalogue, **Art of This Century** (1942), by Peggy Guggenheim. Modified by J. R.

EYE TEST, NOT A "NUDE DESCENDING A STAIRCASE"

> **The**
>
> If you come into * linen, your time is thirsty because * ink saw some wood intelligent enough to get giddiness from a sister; However, even it should be smilable to shut * hair * which * water writes always plural, they have avoided * frequency, *meaning* mother in law; * powder will take a chance; and * road could try. But after somebody brought, any multiplication as soon as * stamp was out, a great many cords refused to go through. Around * wire's people, who will be able to sweeten * rug, *that is to say* ~~it means~~ why must every* patents look for a wife? Pushing four dangers near * listening-place, * vacation had not dug absolutely nor this likeness has eaten.
>
> *remplacer chaque * par le mot: the*

replace each * by the word: *the*

Note. Dated N. Y. October 1915. "The meaning in these sentences was a thing I had to avoid . . . The construction was very painful in a way, because the minute I **did** think of a verb to add to the subject, I would very often see a meaning & immediately I saw a meaning I would cross out the verb & change it . . . until the text would finally read without any echo of the physical world."

RENDEZ-VOUS DU DIMANCHE 6 FEVRIER 1916

-tor. One will be without,at the same time, less than before five elections & also some acquaintance with four little animals; one must occupy this delight so as to decline all responsibility for it. After twelve photos, our hesitation in front of 20 fibers was understandable; even the worst hanging demands good luck corners without counting the prohibition to the linens: How not to marry one's least oculist rather than stand their curls ? No, decidedly, behind your walking-stick marble veining then corkscrew are hidden. However, they confessed, why screw, indispose? The others have mistaken itchings for constructing,in dozens,its lacings. God knows whether we need, although countless eaters,in a subtraction. Truly forbidden therefore, when I will stitch, I say, pra-

-est for profits, in front of which &, as a precaution on purpose,she smashes desserts, even those that it's forbidden to tie. Then, seven or eight poles drink some consequences now appointed; don't forget, by the way, that without stewardship, then with many a similar chance,their huge files return four times; indeed! then,if ferocity merges from behind its own carpet. From tomorrow, at last I'll have put some batteries exactly where several split, accept though they order the periphery. To begin with,did one stick leagues on to bottles,despite their importance in a hundred serenities? A liquid scolding, after denouncing weeks, goes to detest your suitcase, for an edge is enough. ¾At the moment, we are wiped up quite enough, see what a confusion

-ing,after ending your embarrassment. Notwithstanding the fact of six buttons extinguishing one its others (although if, it goes around it)seems to make the buttonholes turn somersaults . A choice remains: long, strong, extendable defections pierced by three worn-out nets, or else, to lay down the only envelope. Have you accepted some sleeves? Could you take his row? Perhpas must we wait for my piling, at the same time, my difficulty; with this kind of things, it's impossible to add an eighth leash. Out of thirty wretched posts, two real ones wish to err, refunded civically, & refuse any compensation out of their sphere. For how long, why how, will this thin water level be limited?   in other words : nails get cold when many finally pleat at last behind , containing

door, from now on in a large quantity will be able to bring out the value of the oblong clan which, without removing any bolster or swinging around fewer bells, will deliver. Only twice every student would like to milk,when ever he facilitates the scatterd see-saw; but, as someone dismantles then gulps down countless dwarf tearings--including oneself--one is olbiged to open up several large clocks so as to obtain an infant drawer. Conclusion: after many an effort in view of the comb, what a pity ! all the furriers have left & mean rice. No question cleans the ignorant or sawn holder;yet given some cages,it had a deep emotion that all the bedridden glues carry out.Uniforms you would have missed if there'd been some pronunciation there

Note. Text, apparently meaningless, typed on four postcards, addressed to Mr. & Mrs. Walter C. Arensberg. Composed under the same conditions as "The" (see above) it reveals a similar impulse toward emptying of the "physical world" & a persistence of meaning as in all of D's work. English version by J. R. utilizing the translation from French in Arturo Schwarz's **Complete Works of Marcel Duchamp.**

MEN BEFORE THE MIRROR

Many a time the mirror imprisons them and holds them firmly. Fascinated they stand in front. They are absorbed, separated from reality and alone with their dearest vice, vanity. However readily they spread out all other vices for all, they keep this one secret and disown it even before their most intimate friends.

There they stand and stare at the landscape which is themselves, the mountains of their noses, the defiles and folds of their shoulders, hands and skin, to which the years have already so accustomed them that they no longer know how they evolved ; and the multiple primeval forests of their hair. They meditate, they are content, they try to take themselves in as a whole. Women have taught them that power does not succeed. Women have told them what is attractive in them, they have forgotten ; but now they put themselves together like a mosaic out of what pleased women in them. For they themselves do not know what is attractive about them. Only handsome men are sure of themselves, but handsome men are not fitted for love : they wonder even at the last moment whether it suits them. Fitted for love are the great ugly things that carry their faces with pride before them like a mask. The great taciturns, who behind their silence hide much or nothing.

Slim hands with long fingers or short, that grasp forth. The nape of a neck that rises steeply to lose itself in the forest's edge of the hair, the tender curve of the skin behind an ear, the mysterious mussel of the navel, the flat pebbles of the knee-caps, the joints of their ankles, which a hand envelops to hold them back from a leap—and beyond the farther and still unknown regions of the body, much older than it, much more worn, open to all happenings : this face, always this face which they know so well. For they have a body only at night and most only in the arms of a woman. But with them goes always, ever present their face.

Note. [From **Marchand du Sel**] "The text is apocryphal & is in effect a literary **ready made.** Composed by a German girlfriend of Man Ray's in her native tongue, then translated into English, it was finally signed by Duchamp qua Rrose Sélavy."

The mirror looks at them. They collect themselves. Carefully, as if tying a cravat, they compose their features. Insolent, serious and conscious of their looks they turn around to face the world.

Rrose Sélavy

From RROSE SÉLAVY

Precision Oculism
RROSE SÉLAVY
New York—Paris
Hairs and Body Blows
all shapes and sizes
*

Rrose Sélavy discovers that an incesticide has to sleep with his mother before killing her; bugs are indispensible.
*

Rrose Sélavy et moi esquivons les ecchymoses des Esquimaux aux mots exquis.
*

Question of personal hygiene :
Should you push the sap of your blade in the lap of your lady?
*

Abominable abdominal furs.
*

Among our other articles of indolent hardware may we recommend this water-tap which stops dripping when you stop listening.
*

Practical fashions, created by Rrose Sélavy:
An oblong gown, designed exclusively for women who suffer from hiccups.
*

Litany of the saints:
I think she must feel from the tips of her tits.
Keep still and you'll feel from the tips of your tits.
How come you feel from the tips of your tits?
I want to feel from the tips of my tits.
*

My niece is cold because my knees are cold.
*

Daily lady cherche demelés avec Daily Mail.

*

Take one cubic centimeter of tobacco smoke and color its outer and
inner surface with a waterproof paint.

*

Sharpen your eye (a form of torture).

*

Opulent alphabets.

*

Anemic cinema.

*

Oh! Do shit again!
Oh! Douche it again!

Note. Originals in French & English. Partially translated by J. R.

ROTATIVE DEMI-SPHERE WITH PUN
AS COVER FOR THE LITTLE REVIEW

THE Bride stripped bare by her bachelors
— (Agricultural machine) — even

(a world in yellow)
preferably in the text ?

In reply to your esteemed letter
of the . . . inst. I have the honor . . .

~~M Duchamp 1913.~~
[this business] has
much to offer . . . .)
not on the title page –

Apparatus
instrument for farming

Kind of Sub-Title
Delay in Glass
Use "delay" instead of "picture" or
"painting"; "picture on glass" becomes
"delay in glass"—but "delay in
glass" does not mean "picture
on glass"—

It's merely a way
of succeeding in no longer thinking
that the thing in question is
a picture—to make a "delay" of it
in the most general way possible,
not so much in the different meanings
in which "delay" can be taken, but
rather in their indecisive reunion
"delay"—a "delay in glass"
    as you would say a "poem in prose"
      or a spittoon in silver

1   1912

The machine with 5 hearts, the pure
child of nickel and platinum must
dominate the Jura-Paris road.
    On the one hand, the chief of the 5 nudes will be
ahead of the 4 other nudes towards this
Jura-Paris road. On the other hand, the headlight
child will be the instrument conquering
this Jura-Paris road
    This headlight child could, graphically,
be a comet, which would have its
tail in front, this tail being an
appendage of the headlight child
appendage which absorbs by
crushing (gold dust, graphically)
this Jura-Paris road.
    The Jura-Paris road, having
to be infinite only humanly,

will lose none of its character of infinity

in finding a termination at one end

in the chief of the 5 nudes, at the other

in the headlight child.

The term "indefinite,, seems to me accurate ^more^

than infinite. The road will begin

in the chief of the 5 nudes. and will not

end in the headlight child.   2

Graphically, this road

will tend towards the pure geometrical line

without thickness (the meeting of 2 planes

seems to me the only pictorial means to achieve

purity)

But in the beginning (in

the chief of the 5 nudes) it will be very finite in

width, thickness ^etc^ , in order little by little,

to become without topographical form in

coming close to this ideal straight line which

finds its opening towards the infinite in the headlight

child.

The pictorial matter of this Jura-Paris road

will be <u>wood</u> which seems to me like

the affective translation of powdered silex.

Perhaps, see if it is necessary to

choose an essence of wood. (the fir tree,

or then polished mahogany)

———————————

Details of execution.

Dimensions.—Plans.

Size of the canvas.

Note: Typographical version by Richard Hamilton. English translation by George Heard Hamilton.

T. S. Eliot

Born 1888 in St. Louis. Died 1965. Williams' description of *The Waste Land* as "the great catastrophe to our letters," along with Eliot's conservatism & the aid & comfort he gave to the academicizers of the 30s & 40s, shouldn't obscure the actual contribution of his work to more extreme, often subterranean developments up to the present. So, for example, the collage techniques of *The Waste Land* (worked out in collaboration with Pound) strikingly pointed, circa 1920, to possibilities for holding multiple experiences in the mind as simultaneity &/or reoccurrence: what he elsewhere called the "simultaneous existence" & "simultaneous order" of all poetries of all times. No question too that he helped to clarify & reinterpret the activity of individual consciousness in the formation of alternative world-images &, as Reznikoff has pointed out, that a *de facto* relation exists between Eliot's "objective correlative," say, & the process of seeing & hearing as key to a felt perception of the world that was at center of "Objectivist" practice, circa 1930, & informs the work of many later poets. And if Eliot himself had to rely on literature & church as props against disorder, the new intuition of poetic origins that he helped develop has led to a more open view of the universally human. His poetry, gathered in *The Complete Poems & Plays*, makes up a tight body of work & has been much anthologized elsewhere, but it may be worth taking a fresh look at the poetics in the context of the propositions in the present volume.

We shall not cease from exploration
And the end of all our exploring
Will be to arrive where we started
And know the place for the first time

AUDITORY IMAGINATION

What I call the "auditory imagination" is the feeling for syllable and rhythm, penetrating far below the conscious levels of thought and feeling, invigorating every word; sinking to the most primitive and forgotten, returning to the origin and bringing something back, seeking the beginning and the end. It works through meanings, certainly, or not without meanings in the ordinary sense, and fuses the old and obliterated and the trite, the current, and the new and surprising, the most ancient and the most civilized mentality.

[From *The Use of Poetry & the Use of Criticism*, 1933]

OBJECTIVE CORRELATIVE

The only way of expressing emotion in the form of art is by finding an "objective correlative"; in other words, a set of objects, a situation, a chain of events which shall be the formula of that *particular* emotion; such that when the external facts, which must terminate in sensory experience, are given, the emotion is immediately evoked.

. . . . .

It is not in his personal emotions, the emotions provoked by particular events in his life, that the poet is in any way remarkable or interesting. His particular emotions may be simple, or crude, or flat. The emotion in his poetry will be a very complex thing, but not with the complexity of the emotions of people who have very complex or unusual emotions in life. One error, in fact, of eccentricity is to seek for new human emotions to express; and in this search for novelty in the wrong place it discovers the perverse. The business of the poet is not to find new emotions, but to use the ordinary ones and, in working them up into poetry, to express feelings which are not in actual emotions at all. And emotions which he has never experienced will serve his turn as well as those familiar to him.

. . . . .

Poetry is not a turning loose of emotion, but an escape from emotion; it is not the expression of personality, but an escape from personality. But, of course, only those who have personality and emotions know what it means to want to escape from these things.

[From *Hamlet*, 1919; & *Tradition & the Individual Talent*, 1919]

Else von Freytag-Loringhoven

Born 1874 in Germany. Died 1927. After World War I she came to the U. S. A. & into association with Duchamp & other N. Y. Dadaists. Regular publication in *The Little Review* established her as the conscious purveyor of a "poetry of madness," a kind of latter-day Rimbaud, only too loud & erotic for a woman, writing in English without a native claim to it, etc. She also did early junk-sculpture & created works of art on her own body, "dressed in rags picked up here and there, decked out with impossible objects suspended from chains, swishing long trains, like an empress from another planet, her head ornamented with sardine cans," to give the appearance of "a Dadaist whimsy, a woman whose whole life was Dada" (G. Hugnet). Only now, after others have practiced similar "transpositions of Dada into daily life," the poetry can be seen not so much as "madness" but as the prophecy of some enormous, often derisive artist turned female-principle. Or as what Djuna Barnes wrote of her, following her return to "mad home & poor house" in Germany & her 1927 death-by-gas in Paris: "In most cases death is neither more nor less than that which we must suffer, in some lonely instances it becomes high tragedy. So it was in her case, because she fought it so knowingly all the latter part of her life, rated it for what it was, feared it, and honored it, adding to it the high tempo of dread and love that set it above her, enormous and evil, by this splendid appraisal." (*Transition*, No. 11, February 1928)

To show hidden beauty of things—there are no limitations!
Only artist can do that—that is his holy office. Stronger—braver
he is—more he will explore into depths.
His eye—ear—finger—nose—tongue—are as keen as yours dull.

Without him—without his help—you would become less than
dog—cow—worm.

To them nature is art—we live in civilization! You would lose
all sense of life—disintegrate into maniacs of wilderness—not into
animals—for: animals are perfect—Nature to them—civilization to us.
1920

AFFECTIONATE

Wheels are growing on rose-bushes
gray and affectionate
O Jonathan—Jonathan—dear
Did some swallow Prendergast's silverheels—
be drunk forever and more
—with lemon appendicitis?

HOLY SKIRTS

Thought about holy skirts—to tune of *"Wheels are growing on
rosebushes."* Beneath immovable—carved skirt of forbidding sex-
lessness—over pavement shoving—gliding—nuns have wheels.

Undisputedly! since—beneath skirts—they are not human!
Kept carefully empty cars—running over religious track—local—
express—according to velocity of holiness through pious steam—up
to heaven!

What for—
what do they unload there—
why do they run?

Senseless wicked expense on earth's provisions—pious idleness—
all idleness unless idleness *before action—idleness of youth!*

Start action upstairs—he?
How able do that—all of sudden—when on earth—machinery
insufficient—weak—unable to carry—virtuous?

Virtue: stagnation.
Stagnation: absent contents—lifeblood—courage—action!
action-n!

Why here?
What here for—?
       To good? ah—!? hurry—speed up—run amuck—jump—
beat it! farewell! fare-thee-well—good-bye! bye!
ah—bye-ye-ye!

We—of this earth—like this earth!
make heaven here—
take steps here—
to possess bearing hereafter—
dignity.

That we know how to enter:
reception room—drawing room—
banquet hall of:
abyssmal serious jester
whimsical serene power!
Poke ribs:
old son of gun—
old acquaintance!
Kiss: knees—toes!
Home—!
Our home!
We are home!
After:
smiling grim battle—
laughter—excitement—
swordplay—
sweat—
blood— —!
After accomplishing—
what sent for to accomplish.
Children of His loin—
Power of power.

THE LITTLE REVIEW

MINESELF—MINESOUL—AND—MINE—CAST-IRON LOVER

by Else Baroness von Freytag–Loringhoven

Mine Soul Singeth—Thus Singeth. Mine Soul—This Is What Mine Soul Singeth:

His hair is molten gold and a red pelt—
His hair is glorious!

Yea—mine soul—and he brushes it and combeth it—he maketh
it shining and glistening around his head—and he is vain about
it—but alas—mine soul—his hair is without sense—his hair
does not live—it is no revelation, no symbol! HE is not gold—
not animal—not GOLDEN animal—he is GILDED animal only—
mine soul! his vanity is without sense—it is the vanity of one who
has little and who weareth a treasure meaningless! O—mine soul
—THAT soulless beauty maketh me sad!

"His nostrils"—singeth mine soul —"his nostrils!" seeest thou not
the sweep of the scythe with which they curveth up his cheek
swiftly?

Iron—mine soul—cast-iron! his nostrils maketh me sad! there is
no breath of the animal that they may quiver? they do not curve
swiftly—the scythe moveth—mine soul—they are still—they are
motionless like death! NOT like death—in death has been life—
they are iron—mine soul—cast-iron! a poor attempt to picture
life—a mockery of life—as I see cast-iron animals and monuments
a mockery of life— — alas—mine soul—HIS soul is cast-iron!
"Iron" singeth mine soul—"iron thou canst hammer with strength—
iron thou canst shape—bend—iron thou canst make quiver—iron

alive to flame— —
ART THOU FLAME?"

Mine soul—alas—I COULD BE!
And WHY—mine body—dost thou say: "I COULD BE" and
WHY—mine body—dost thou ALL THE WHILE SAY:
"ALAS"? Thine "ALAS" maketh me sad!

Mine soul dost not be mischievious! THOU KNOWEST we are
One—thou knowest thou ART flame! it is THOU—mine soul—
and thine desire to flare by thineself which maketh thine body
say: "alas"! thou hast so changed! dost thou not hinder mine
wish to touch—mine right since olden times which was granted
me ever? because thou art now very strong—I gave thee much
fuel—NOW—mine soul—thou art stronger than I and thou
mocketh thine body! and—mine soul—are we artisans—are we not
artists who flare by themselves—FOR themselves? we do not bend
any more out of our way to catch and touch—to mold be molded—
to feed be fed — — we flare HIGH—mine soul—we are SATIS-
FIED! — — —

And yet—mine body—thou sayest "alas"!
Ha—mine soul—I say "alas" and I say "alas" and "alas" and
"alas"! because I am thine BODY! and this is mine flaming de-
sire to-day: that he shall step into THEE through ME as it was
in olden times and that we will play again that old WONDERFUL
play of the "TWOTOGETHER"!— —mine soul—if thus it will
be—willst thou flare around him—about him—over him—hide
him with shining curtain — — — hiss that song of savage joy—
starry-eyes — — willst thou heat—melt—make quiver—break
down—dissolve—build up — — SHAKE HIM—SHAKE HIM—
SHAKE HIM—O mine starry-eyed soul?

Heia! ja-hoho! hisses mine starry-eyed soul in her own language.

I see mine soul—we still understand each other! I LOVE THEE
thou very great darling! we must wait and smile — — — PER-
HAPS SARDONICALY — — — mine very great soul — — —
because we now are artists — — — and: NOTHING
MATTERS ! ! !

Mineself—Minesoul—Arguing

Minesoul—why hast thou awakened thine body with thine great

song? now I am desirous for possession!

Mine body thou art wrong—THOU madest sing mine song—thine eyes are mine fingers—THEY TOUCH! guard thine eyes mine body guard thine sensual eyes!

Mine soul—HOW?—shall I go blind—senseless? I see—I smile— I suffer! I MUST TOUCH! HERE MINE EYES—HERE MINE HANDS! why not— wise soul? am I not child—playfull—full of laughter? it is not mine wish to smile sardonicaly—THOU— mine soul—smileth thus—thou dost not wish thine body to touch —thou giveth up beforehand—surrender to keep thine body— surrender to NOTHINGNESS! thou art jealous!!

Alas—mine soul—thou maketh me sad—thou maketh sad thine body! thou maketh me smile sad lying smile—smile triumphant in emptiness! it is NOT the smile of thine body—THOU art wise —mine soul—not thine body—I am tired of thee—let me go! alas—mine soul I AM TIRED OF WISDOM!

Art not thine eyes mine fingers—mine body—did they not touch until they form his image in me?

IMAGE IN THEE? I DO NOT WANT IMAGE!!! here are MINE fingers—mine soul—alas—mine soul—here are MINE FINGERS! MINE FINGERS SUFFER—! they are MINE eyes —their touch is SIGHT—mine fingers wish to touch—caress— mine fingers will caress with soft pious look — — — look full of laughter — — — look full of motion —• — — look full of dizziness —insanity — — which maketh steady and sane— — —maketh steady and sane thine body!
Alas—mine soul—thine body is shaky—the fingers of thine body squint!
They are filled with tears—´— —they are BLIND!

Alas—mine body—use thine fingers desirous to see! pray—caress —flame—burn deep—mark the place— — — —dance in laughter and dizziness— — —come back with fingers strong—steady—wise —shining stars!

Go—give and take!— — —alas—mine body—thou maketh me sad!

Mine soul—mine soul—is it not so — — — alas—mine soul— is it not so— — —mine eyes—thine fingers—grew unsteady—dim

—limp— — —

Mine body—thou maketh me sad— — —thou VERILY hast
made sad—thine soul — — —! mine body—alas—I bid thee
—GO!!!

THOU—mine soul?!
I—mine body.

Heia!—mine soul—hoho!—brave soul—but—alas—strong soul—
I have no wings—no money! thine body stayed poor in giving
treasures to thee;—now thou art weak—I weakened thee with
mine desires! thou art filled with treasures — — — thou willst
break! thou art supple—not robust — — — from childhood I
know thee! let us be strong together with strength of the last!!!
hast thou teeth? bite into MINE flesh I will bite into THINE!
—we totter—but will not drop! — — — WE MUST WAIT
AND SMILE—mine soul—in waiting thus not can I smile very
much any more—nor successfully thine sardonical smile—it died from
emptiness—our triumph was rash—I deceived thee—smiling thus!
I am thine body—mine soul—thine REVOLTING body ! ! ! let
us have understanding:

There is no touch — — — ALL OUR FINGERS SUFFER! there
is no sight — — — — ALL OUR EYES SUFFER! — — — —
let me sing that song of what mine eyes saw—thine fingers touched
—our senses remember! — — — let me sinr MINE song after
thine ! ! !

I Sing Mine Soul—Thus I Sing—Mine Soul—This is What I Sing Mine Soul:

Frail steeltools—reddish complexion—pale ivory — — — talons—
finely chiseled—finely carved animal!
Thus his hands—I saw his hands—I love his hands—I believe in
hands—mine soul!

ANIMAL—mine body—CAST-IRON ANIMAL?
CHISELLED animal—mine soul aloof — — — —! those hands
LIVE—never came to life— — —are afraid—never were BORN!

I touch them:— — —they quiver!
I kiss them:— — —they grasp—clutch—tear—draw blood —

— —Steeltools—reddish complexion—chiseled talons—carved animal—pale animal—caveanimal—animal of shadow — — —! it blushes CRIMSON around its edges—around its edges it runs over with crimson — — — its ears shells before flame! — — — THUS I know it to be!

"THUS thou knowest it to be" — — —! dost thou know his heart—mine body?
NEVER— — —! mine soul!

He should NOT be crimson around his edges—nor shell before flame! in the MIDDLE should he be crimson — — — HEART flare crimson — — — ears crimsoned by heartsblood!!! will he wear crimson flame like star in his middlechest — — — or willst thou hold him before thee—pale—lifeless—to SHINE THROUGH HIS LIFELESSNESS ONLY — — — mine body?

MINE SOUL—MINE SOUL—thou maketh me shiver — — — thus can it not be! dost thou remember that song of his hair which made mine eyes thine fingers?

Thine eyes made mine song—mine body—thine eyes TOUCH! guard thine eyes—mine body—guard thine sensual eyes!

Sing thine sensual song—mine soul— — —thus it ran:

"HIS HAIR IS MOLTEN GOLD AND A RED PELT — — — HIS HAIR IS GLORIOUS! — — — —"
Thou hast strong colorsense—mine body—thou loveth red!—thou paint pale animal crimson!

IT *IS* CRIMSON! I paint pale animal with its crimson blood! to arouse it I will probe deep; should it have no blood?

I must kiss his hands—mine soul—his hands to arouse crimson—crimson in reddish pale palms—violet veins of his temples—he will run over with crimson — — —! crimson lamp of ivory—shell with heart of flame!

SEEEST HIS NOSTRILS—mine soul—shining with crimson—flaring with breath?, — — — — THE SCYTHE MOVETH!—crimson scythe—bloody scythe—curving up his cheek swiftly ! ! !

MINE SOUL—SO BEAUTIFUL HE IS ! ! !

EYES— — —golden eyes of the toad!
Sawest thou eyes—mine body?
I saw HIS eyes—mine soul—hidden behind shining surfaces of
glass!

He is hidden like the hidden toad — — — hidden animal—cave-
animal—chiseled animal—animal of shadow! — — goldrimmed
pupils narrowing in light—blinking—thinking dark dreams!
Hidden—lightshy—skinpale—does not perish in flame—I remem-
ber old witchword;
Jewels hidden in its head— — —hidden—hidden—hidden animal?
Splendid—proud—majestic—immobile— — —when it feeds it
moveth swift like thought!
Eyes closing in passion—opening—not knowing passion—bowels
dancing—eyes stony jewels in its head!
The toad—proud—majestic—immobile—never treacherous — —
— should it not be loved?
I love the majestic toad—feel ashamed before its mastery of emo-
tion—scarcety of motion! I gaze into its stony eyes—goldrimmed
glimmering—centerdark—with mystery of dark honest dreams—
— — thinking heavily—unwinkingly!

MINE SOUL—TOAD HE IS — — — yet he does not DARE
TO BE TOAD! HIDDEN IN HIMSELF—HIDDEN FROM
HIMSELF—HIDDEN ANIMAL!
Toadsoul hidden by glare of roadside; — — —
thinking himself a BEE ! ! !

fluttering like bee—on roadside!
toadeyes hidden by shining surfaces of glass!
not to blink on roadside like toad!

flutter he must—squirm—smile—polite smile of bees and multi-
tude—to find food—not to be exposed a toad—toadking— — —
thinking dark dreams behind shining surfaces of glass!

ALAS—MINE SOUL—HE IS NOT HAPPY!

Mobile he is—not immobile! fidgety—not majestic! usurperpride
—full of suspicious fear—looking for disrespect! STIFF pride—
not proud enough — — — such pride is his!

No certainty of station—quietness of inheritance! no ease—dignity—serenity—aloofness!
Much restless fidgeting there is!
He has no rest!
Feeds too much—moveth too much—turns—bows his head too often—smileth—strained smile of bees and multitude.
His shellpale skin—his goldrimmed eyes ITCH with pain of light!
Cry out for darkness—shadow—mystery—loneliness— —dreams —TOADDREAMS!
Should eat less—dream more—alas—mine soul—he does not know—has not found out—not found' his toad-nature!
Young and human he is — — — HUMANS FIND THEIR PLACES WITH THEIR BRAINS!
In glasshouse he sits—not in cave—fire he fears!
IMMUNITY FROM FIREDEATH is not his knowledge—nor flame as pleasure to skin!
MAY SQUAT IN CENTER OF CRIMSON THRONE — CRIMSON HE—CRIMSON CROWN—KING IN STATE—UNBLINKING!

THINKETH HIMSELF A BEE!
LIVETH a bee—liveth WITH bees— in hustle—on roadside!
Every day shrinketh from light—chiselled lips twitching—
toadeyes hidden behind shining surfaces of glass!
HIS CROWN HE WEARETH BOLDLY ON ROADSIDE—in hustle—in dust—in glare— — —his crown he weareth SHAMELESSLY!
SO MUCH he dareth to differ from bees—to be costly— —not TOO costly! not to be exiled—a toad—TOADKING!
Weareth his crown without magnitude—solitude—a trinket—a LITTLE thing!
Thinking himself GOLDEN BEE—at UTMOST—thinking himself costly—not too costly — — — not to arouse Beehatred!
WITHOUT BEES feareth loneliness—famine — — — covering every day little golden trinket with little black hat!
Thus the custom of bees;
Chiselled lips harden—shellpale skin coarsens—toadblood OOZES in reddish pale palms—sweating—crying for darkness—crimson—solitude!
BLOODRIGHT — — — BLOODWISHES — — — he does not know!
Weareth the stamp of the toad and the king upon his head in broad daylight—thinking it a trinket to be costly before bees!

Covering with little black hat every day → — — A CROWN!

YEA — — — HE DOES NOT LOOK COSTLY TO THINE
BODY — — — ALAS—mine soul—not THAT WAY!
Costly he looketh a toad—creature that IS—demands bloodright
and balance — — — has it—finds it—SQUATS on it!
Costly he looketh in grandeur—magnitude—eyes stony—darkcen-
terd — — — gazing undisturbed at good and evil for him — — —
thinking ceaselessly — — — unwinkingly — — — dreams —
TOADDREAMS!
SQUATING IN SHADOW DARKNESS UPON CENTER
OF CRIMSON THRONE — — — SQUATING CON-
TENTEDLY — FEEDING SWIFTLY — EYES CLOSING IN
PASSION—OPENING NOT KNOWING PASSION—BOWELS
DANCING—EYES STONY JEWELS IN ITS HEAD!
TOADKING!
BEE IS BEE — — — TOAD IS TOAD — — — WE — MINE
SOUL — THE CRIMSON THRONE!
FROM US NO TOAD SHRINKETH — — — JUMPETH AWAY
—SHRIEKING! UPON US IT JUMPETH — — — SQUATETH
—BASKETH!
FROM US NO *TOADKING SHRINKETH ! ! !*

Patient soul—dost thou notice — — —: he is curious?
Smelleth smoke—suspecteth flame—draweth near— — —jumpeth
far?
TOADBLOOD STIRRING — — — BEESENSE SHRIEK-
ING!
TOAD HE IS— — —thrown young onto bees at roadside!— — —
fearing its element!

MINE PROUD SOUL— — —is he crippled—DISGUISED TO
HIMSELF ONLY? NOT is he disguised to thine body—nor
—wise patient soul—to THEE!
WILL PUT HIM UPON CENTER OF CRIMSON THRONE
—SHALL SQUAT AND BASK — — — OR PERISH AND
BURN!
THINE BODY AND THOU—MINE SOUL—WE DO NOT
LIKE CRIPPLES!
UPRIGHT WE STAND — — — SLANDER WE FLARE
— — — THINE BODY AND THOU—MINE SOUL — — —
HISSING!—

THUS—MINE SOUL—IS MINE SONG TO THEE— — ---THUS
ITS END.

Marsden Hartley

Born 1877 in Lewiston, Maine. Died in Ellsworth, Maine in 1943. His work, both as painter & poet, moved between abstraction & attachment to locality & the "secret sacred rite of/love of place." First show, 1909, through Stieglitz's Gallery 291; lived in Europe (but especially Germany) from 1912 to 1916, where he met Gertrude Stein, the Cubists, etc., & came under the influence of painters like Marc & Kandinsky. On return to America he connected with the Others group & New York Dada; wrote of that time: "I am come to the clearest point of my vision, which is nothing more or less than the superbly enlightening discovery that life as we know it is an essentially comic issue and cannot be treated other than with the spirit of comedy in comprehension. . . . Dada is a fundamentally religious attitude, analogous to that of the scientist with his eyeglass glued to the microscope. . . . Dada destroys and stops at that. Let Dada help us to make a complete clearance, then each of us rebuild a modern house with central heating, and everything to the drain, Dadas of 1920." His early writings appeared in magazines like *291*, *Camera Work*, *Others*, *Rongwrong*, *Dadaglobe*, *N.Y. Dada*, & in *25 Poems* (Contact Editions, 1923). Later books included *Androscoggin* (1923) & *Selected Poems* (1945).

. . . There is an inner substance, an inner content in all things—an interior in an interior, an exterior to an exterior—and there are forms for the expression of them. It is the artist's business to select forms suitable to his own specialized experience, forms which express naturally the emotions he personally desires to present, leaving conjectures and discussions to take care of themselves. They add nothing to art. . . . True modes of art are derived from individuals

understanding life. The idea of modernity is but a new attachment to things universal—a fresh relationship to the course of the sun and to the living swing of the earth—a new fire of affection and the living essence present everywhere. The new wonder of the moment. The Creator never loses his sense of wonder—he is continually in the state of simple amaze. The delight which exists in ordinary moments is his ecstasy. . . .
1914

LOCAL BOYS AND GIRLS SMALL TOWN STUFF

A panther sprang at the feet
Of the young deer in the grey wood.
It was the lady who had sworn
To love him,
That rose, wraithlike
From the flow of his blood.
He swooned with her devotions.

There was never one
More jolly and boyish
Than he was, in the great beginning.
Once his slippers were fastened
With domesticity,
He settled down
Like a worn jaguar
Weary with staring through bars.
The caresses that were poured
Over his person
Staled on him.
Love had grown rancid.
Have you emptied the garbage
John?

Prometheus fire
Never can worship
The smell of hams and hocks
Issuing from the smokehouse.
The odours of the street
Hold enticements
That bear entertaining.
There is at least
The tincture of virility
Present.

From "1920-1922"
In confidence with those well —

                  remaining kings —

it will not be selfish
        of any of us
            to agree
      with the Bishop of Manchester
      that a man may be
          merely
a mollusc — a forked radish —
the eye of an ancient cactus root
        yearning toward Madrid —
It would be unkind of us
          only
   to think he has made an
        apocryphal
           error
     in his otherwise
        impeccably
          discriminative
            judgment,

these being bishops,
    being noted for their powers
    in proferring first hand —

second, heavy handed
> *information*
about the species in general.
The CENOTAPH *would have another*
> > *wooden wreath*
if the heresy of this suggestion
> *were proven......*

· · · · · ·

YOURS WITH DEVOTION
trumpets and drums
Dearest Saltimbanques —
> *beatrice — muriel —*
> > > *mary —*
> *shaw — not garden —*
> > *" when they go the other way"*
> > OTHER WAY *— dearest — ;*
> > > REMEMBER —
Mary so knowing — emma — emily —
> > > *beatrice — muriel —*
> *bandwaggon of heavenly saltimbanques —*
yes yes — girlies — performance at eleven in the late afternoon —
> *wires all spread — canvas — stretched*
special thunderstorm to be pulled — for YOU — for YOU —
and YOU — and YOU — and YOU —
> *saltimbanques come straight from HEAven —*
Toto — ella — and ethel —
french nacre — frigidity english —
ALL — ALL — ALL — ALL — ALL —
> *hurdygurdy-merrygoround —*
Offset of delicious word DISGUST —
> *saltimbanques are from Heaven —*
eh bien TOTO — et toi — ELLA — so murderously
aware — IMPECCABLE ELLA — BERtie —
> > *having given us*
> > > *to feel*
> *the difficulties of*

> SNIPESHOOTING *in the gutters of the*
> STRAND —

with a prince albert to cover those votive limbs
> hungrier for chops — than for the immoral
> > NUdeness of the TRuth —

shall we invite minnie — that one who had the courage —
> > to run —

the gamut — from hedda to hannele —
> never — glorious one — having to my knowledge
> > taken advantage of any innocent word in our
> > novel SPEECH —

and lily ?

> > lena, naturellement —
> > > most perfect legs since Pauline Hall
> > > so the old ducks say.

> shall we phone for lily ?
> saltimbanques are from HEAVEN —
> > c'est tout — ma chère —

TOTO — pav —
> WATTS — Pav —
give us these gentlemen pavs — who turn PIROUETTES
> into handsprings — standing upon skates
> > of wood — and upon
> > muscles of chalcedony —

saltimbanques are from heaven —
> beatrice — and muriel —
> > astarte of the SKATING rink —
> > > juno of the TIGHT wire —

puppets pull their own strings if having the
> > intelligence — of bea —
> > and muri —
> > they pull them well —
> > > WELL — I said —
> > > W-E-L-L —

saltimbanques are from HEAven —
> franklin and CHarles — muscles — muscles — muscles —
> george and dicky — lines — lines — lines —
> saltimbanques are from HEAven —

Experience — without — expurgation —
              everyone's rabelaisian step-parent —
              everyone dammed by mrs. beterouge —
I have a thousand mouchoirs —

                              Phyllis and Philippe —
send us many another bandwaggon, GOD —
        filled with saltimbanques like
              FRanklin and CHarles —
                    and TOTO — and ETHEL — and ELLA —
you have heard what I said —
        SALTIMBANQUES ARE STRAIGHT
                                    from heaven —

              That's all, infinitely all —
                    That's all —
                        ALL.
                                ALL.
                                ALL.
dance hellions, all of you —
                        for you very lives —

              •   •   •   •   •   •

MEDIOCRITY
        I have come to admire
              it is so plentiful
                    as I watch
                        the squirmings
                                        of
                        these unattached searchers
                            after spurious elegance
              I say to myself
                    how beautiful is a derrick —
                        it hoists actualities upon—
                            a plan of
                                    measurable height —

SWISH SWISH SWISH
                on a sandboard
                        to waltztime
                            in the flare
                            of a white SPOT
                                illumining
                                        most splendidly.

MEDIOCRITY
            is so stimulating —
                    naturally not the
                            copycattish
                                mediocrity of
                                        arrivistiv talentry

        but RATHER
                the calm mediocrity of
                    the battered
                                TOMASSO
                    sleeping on a heap of ashes
                in an overloaded receptacle of degenerated
                                        domestic
                                    OFFAL.

It is by means of TOMASSO
                        laziness
                            vivid night
                                in wind-torn
                                        airshafts and
                                            reprobatish
                                                cellars

in quest of
                reciprocal antagonism
                        perfected mediocrity
                                            is permitted
        not with that copycatting of the well trained
                                    parrot
                                above a most tiresome
                                            fishglobe.

I say so too, Monsieur Coalfleet
            or if you prefer it, Pierre —

isn't it simply
                    to howl
like a coyote

                    against the dizzy night
when you know
                    that the giant of
                            twenty-four
who sits there
        sipping coffee
        smoking a pipe
            like a
                MAN —
        made for the
                    chopping down
                    of worn-out
                            useless
                                centuries

        spends his
                best hours
                        beating eggs
        for an
                OMELETTE SURPRISE
Hegel
        Kant
            Schopenhauer
                        take notice —
is there
        really
                nothing
                    to
                    be
                        done
for the
        prevention
                of cruelty
        to one's
                priceless

                        sense
                        of humour ?
I do not wonder
        that members

                of the best families
                        among
                                the centuries
        burst a
                vessel
                        and pass
                        AWAY
        now
            and
                    then
        out
                of
                    helpless   HYSTERIA.

Mina Loy

Born 1883 in England. Died 1966 in Aspen, Colorado. Her work started to appear circa 1913, & by 1918, Pound (probably unaware she was an Englishwoman) reviewed her & Marianne Moore as "a distinctively national product . . . something which could not have come out of any other country," & which, he said, typified the process he called *logopoeia* or "poetry that is akin to nothing but language, which is a dance of the intelligence among words and ideas and modification of ideas and characters." His further description of it, "the utterance of clever people in despair, or hovering upon the brink of that precipice," now seems more true of Loy than Moore; & what he fails to observe on Loy's side is that her work by 1918 had taken on a largeness of theme & an energy of sound & image that few in her generation could match. By then too, or soon thereafter, she was into a private mythology, *Anglo-Mongrels & the Rose*, that the present editor finds comparable to, & probably not chronologically behind, Pound's early *Cantos* & Eliot's *Waste Land*. But the parts ended up scattered like the limbs of Osiris, & by the time a few fragments turned up under other titles in Jargon Press' expanded reprint of her selected poems, *Lunar Baedeker* (1958), none of the three poets introducing the book (William Carlos Williams, Kenneth Rexroth & Denise Levertov) could recall the large work from which they came. So, if anyone wants to take the hint & read through *Rogue, Broom, The Little Review, Others, Contact*, etc., they may be able to piece together one of the lost master-poems of the 20th century.

and so they have

THE mind is a magician bound by assimilations; let him loose and the smallest idea conceived in freedom will suffice to negate the wisdom of all forefathers.
*

YOU cannot restrict the mind's capacity.
THEREFORE you stand not only in abject servitude to your perceptive consciousness—
BUT also to the mechanical re-actions of the subconsciousness, that rubbish heap of race-tradition—
AND believing yourself free—your least conception is colored by the pigment of retrograde superstitions.
*

TO your blushing we shout the obscenities, we scream the blasphemies that you, being weak, whisper alone in the dark,
THEY are empty except of your shame
AND so these sounds shall dissolve back to their innate senselessness.
THUS shall evolve the language of the Future.

From "Aphorisms on Futurism," 1914

LOVE SONGS

I

Spawn of fantasies
Sifting the appraisable
Pig Cupid   his rosy snout
Rooting erotic garbage
"Once upon a time"
Pulls a weed   white star-topped
Among wild oats sown in mucous membrane
I would   an eye in a Bengal light
Eternity in a sky-rocket
Constellations in an ocean
Whose rivers run no fresher
Than a trickle of saliva

These are suspect places

I must live in my lantern
Trimming subliminal flicker
Virginal   to the bellows
Of experience
                    Colored glass.

V

Shuttle-cock and battle-door
A little pink-love
And feathers are strewn

VIII

Midnight empties the street
                To the left a boy
   One wing has been washed in the rain
   The other will never be clean any more—
Pulling door-bells to remind
Those that are snug
                To the right a haloed ascetic
                Threading houses
Probes wounds for souls
—The poor can't wash in hot water—
And I don't know which turning to take—

IX

We might have coupled
In the bed-ridden monopoly of a moment
Or broken flesh with one another
At the profane communion table
Where wine is spill't on promiscuous lips
We might have given birth to a butterfly
With the daily-news
Printed in blood on its wings

COSTA MAGIC

                    Her father
Indisposed to her marriage
And a rabid man at that
My most sympathetic daughter
Make yourself a conception
As large as this one
Here
But with yellow hair

From the house
Issuing   Sunday dressed
Combed precisely
                    Splosh!
Pours something
Viscous
Malefic
Unfamiliar

While listening up   I hear my husband
Mumbling   Mumbling
Mumbling   at the window
    Malediction
    Incantation

Under an hour
Her hand to her side pressing
Suffering
Being bewitched
Cesira fading
Daily   daily   feeble   softer

The doctor   "Pthisis"
The wise woman says to take her
So we   following her instruction
I and the neighbour
Take her

The glass rattling
The rain slipping
I and the neighbour and her aunt
Bunched together
And Cesira
Droops across the cab

Fields and houses
Pass   like the pulling out
Of sweetmeat ribbon
From a rascal's mouth
Till
A wheel in a rut
Jerks back my girl on the padding

And the hedges into the sky

Coming to the magic tree

Cesira becomes as a wild beast
                    A tree of age

"If Cesira should not become as a wild beast
It is merely Pthisis"
This being the wise woman's instruction

Knowing she has to die
We drive home
To wait
She certainly does in time

It is unnatural in a Father
Bewitching a daughter
whose hair   down   covers her thighs

ANGLO-MONGRELS AND THE ROSE (Part One)

EXODUS lay under an oak-tree
 Bordering on Buda Pest he had lain
 him down to over-night under the lofty rain
 of starlight
 having leapt from the womb
eighteen years ago and grown
neglected along the shores of the Danube
on the Danube in the Danube
-or breaking his legs behind runaway horses-
 with a Carnival quirk
 every Shrove Tuesday

X X X

 Of his riches
 a Patriarch
 erected a synagogue
 - -for the people
His son
looked upon Lea
- - of the people
 she sat in Synagogue
 -her hair long as the Talmud
 -her tamarind eyes- -
and disinherited
begat this Exodus

Imperial Austria taught the child
the German secret patriotism
the Magyar tongue the father
stuffed him with biblical Hebrew and the
seeds of science exhorting him
 to vindicate
 his forefather's ambitions

The child
flowered precociously fever
smote the father

the widowed mother
took to her bosom   a spouse
of her own sphere
and hired
Exodus in apprenticeship
to such   as garrulously inarticulate
ignore   the cosmic cultures

Sinister foster-parents
who lashed the boy
to that paralysis of
the spiritual apparatus
common to
the poor
The arid gravid
intellect   of jewish ancestors
        the senile juvenile
        calculating prodigies of Jehovah
        -Crushed by the Occident ox
        they scraped
        the gold gold golden
        muck from off its hoofs-

moves Exodus   to emmigrate
        coveting the alien
        asylum   of voluntary military
        service   paradise   of the pound-stirling
        where the domestic Jew   in lieu
        of knouts   is lashed with tongues

X   X   X

   The cannibal God
shutters his lids of night   on the day's gluttony
the partially   devoured humanity
warms its unblessed beds   with bare prostrations
An insect   from an herb
errs on the   man-mountain

imparts   its infinitesimal tactile stimulus
to the epiderm   to the spirit
of Exodus
stirring   the anaesthetised load
of racial instinct frustrated
impulse   infantile impacts with unreason
      on his unconscious

      Blinking his eyes-   - -
         at sunrise   Exodus
lumbar-aching   sleep logged   turns his ear
to the grit earth   and hears
the boom of cardiac cataracts
         thumping the turf
with his young pulse

He is undone!   How should he know
he has a heart   The Danube
gives no instruction in anatomy-
the primary
throb of the animate
a beating mystery
pounds on his ignorance
in seeming
death dealing-

      The frightened fatalist
      clenches his eyes
      for the involuntary sacrifice
      stark
      to the sun-zumm dirges of
      a bee
      he lays him out
      for his heart-beats to slay him

It is not accomplished
the burning track
of lengthening sun shafts
spur

This lying-in-state of a virility
to rise
and in his surprised
protracted viability
    shoulder his pack

Exodus   whose initiations
in arrogance   through brief
stimulation of his intellect
in servitude   through early
ill-usage   etch involute
inhibitions
upon his sensibility

sharpened and blunted   he
-bound for his unformulate
conception of life-
makes for the harbour

and the   dogged officer of Destiny
    kept Exodus
and that which he begat
moving along

The highest paid   tailor's
cutter in the 'City'
Exodus   Lord Israel
nicknamed   from his consummate bearing
his coaly eye
challenging   the unrevealed universe
speaking fluently   'business-English'
to the sartorial world

jibbering   stock exchange quotations
and conundrums of finance
to which   unlettered immigrants are instantly
initiate
    Those foreigners
before whom   the soul

of the new Motherland
stands nakedly incognito
in so many ciphers

In the boarding-house   the lady with
the locket   "You will excuse me-   -
Our Dear Queen   picks chicken bones in
her fingers"   Exodus   at leisure
painting   knowing not why
sunflowers turned sunwards

Sundays   when
England closed   the eyes of every
commercial enterprise
but the church   and spewed
her silent servants   out of her areas
in their bi-weekly 'best'   to
"Ow get along with you"   their lurching lovers
along the rails of parks
The high-striped   soldiers of the swagger-stick
tempting the wilder flowers of womanhood
to lick-be-quick ice cream
outside the barracks

This jovian hebrew 'all dressed up'
and nowhere to go'
stands like a larch
upon the corners of incarcerate streets
deploring the anomolous legs
of Zion's sons
with the subconscious
irritant of superiority
left in an aristocacy   out of currency

paces
the cancellated desert of the metropolis
with the instinctive urge   of loneliness
to get to 'the heart of something'

The heart of England
sporting its oak
on the rude ratepayer
Hymns   ancient and modern
bela bour   crippled cottage-grands
in parlour fronts
        A thrush
shatters its song upon the spurious shade
of a barred bird-fancier's
The dumb philosophies
of the wondering jew
fall into rhythm   with
long unlistened-to   hebrew chants
        A wave
'out of tide'   with the surrounding
ocean   he breaks
insensitized   non-participance   upon himself

(The) unperceived
conqueror   of a new world
in terms of cutting and drafting
        Exodus   lifts his head
over the alien crowds
under the alien clouds
proudly   as memory
evokes   the panic-stricken
discoverer of his own heart   coming
barefoot   to the Synagogue
erected by his grandfather   -   -   -
The Rabbi said "Your grandfather
was a great and a   just man
we reap what he has sown
- honoured be his memory   so here's
your fare   third class
        May the God of Israel
        bless thee among the Gentiles"

And the God of the Gentiles
blessed him among Israel

he had several
shares in the South Eastern
Railway   and other
securities   Suddenly

he remembers   how his mother
told him   he was a seven month's child
-thing of etherial circulation-
wrapped in wadding   somewhat
green-seeming   as an untimely apple
And Exodus   feels cold
with sympathy   for that cold thing
that was himself - - -
The london dusk
wraps up the aborted entity
heeding Solomon's admonishing   spends
circumcised   circumspect
his evenings   doing lightening calculations
for his high pleasure   Painting - - -
feeling his pulse - - -

                    Incorporeal express trains
from opposite directions
of unequal   lengths and velocities
flash   through his abstract eye
determines instantly   the time
to a decimal   fraction of a second
they take   to pass each other

Under his ivory hands
his sunflowers sunwards
glow   confuse   with itinerant
Judaic eyes   peering
through narrow-slim   entrance-arches
The terrestrial trees   shades
virgin bosoms and blossoms
in course of his acclimatization
a hedge-rose - - - -

He paints
He feels his pulse

The spiritual   tentacles of vanity
that each   puts out towards   the culture
of his epoch   knowing not how to find
and finding not   contact   he has repealed
to fumble among his guts

The only
personal reality
he brought from Hungary   he takes
to Harley street   where medicine
sits   the only   social science   applied to the outsider

- - - - -

The parasite   attaches to the English Rose
- - - - - at a guinea a visit
   becomes   more tangible to himself   the exile
mechanism   he learns   is built
to the same osseous structure   shares
identical phenomena   with those
populating the Island
            that segregated
from his apprehension   moves
a universe   of unceasing
energies   for the biological
explorer's introspection

His body
becomes the target of his speculation

His brain   ranvenous for informative food
spins   cobwebs   on the only available
branching out of facts
clings   to the visceral

items   he has heard mentioned
          until they ache
under mesmeric concentration
Exodus   discovers his nerves
as once   Mankind
in pathological mysticism   believed
itself   to have discovered
its soul
David's daughter's doweries
and olive-eyes
virgins capitalized
to tantalize!

Jehovah's tailor

sets up in business for himself
however
Some queer
marital independence on the English air
keeping him bachelor

While through
stock quotations
and Latin prescriptions
for physic
filters the lyric
aroma of the rose

Exodus knows
no longer father
or brother
or the God of the Jews,
it is his to choose
finance or
romance of the rose

Marianne Moore

Born 1887 in St. Louis. Died 1972. A brilliant, often far-out collagist, she enlarged the range of incorporation & the limits of "personality" in the poem. Though she would later deny the relation of her work to other avant garde propositions, her early poem on poetry, "I too dislike it" (amplified in subsequent 1961 interview to: "what I write could only be called poetry because there is no other category in which to put it"), adopts a strategy not far from Duchamp's proposal to "make works which are not 'works of art.' " (Compare, e.g., her stripping-in of "business documents & schoolbooks" with Duchamp's "ready-mades," etc.) In "An Octopus," below, the raw materials, mostly set off in quotes, include bits from the *London Graphic* & the *Illustrated London News*, Clifton Johnson's *What to See in America*, W. D. Wilcox's *The Rockies of Canada*, W. D. Hyde's *The Five Great Philosophies*, & John Ruskin, John Muir, Cardinal Newman, & *The National Parks Portfolio* (U. S. Department of the Interior Rules & Regulations). "Hence," she said elsewhere, "my writing is, if not a cabinet of fossils, a kind of collection of flies in amber."

Marianne Moore came to New York City circa 1916 & lived there until her death. The association with Williams & Pound dates from that time also, & from 1925 to 1929, she was editor of *The Dial*. Earlier books included *Poems* (Egoist Press, 1921), *Observations* (1924), *Selected Poems* (1935), *What Are Years?* (1941), & *Nevertheless* (1944), selections from which appear in *The Complete Poems of Marianne Moore* (1967).

AN OCTOPUS

of ice. Deceptively reserved and flat,
it lies "in grandeur and in mass"
beneath a sea of shifting snow dunes;
dots of cyclamen-red and maroon on its clearly defined pseudopodia
made of glass that will bend—a much needed invention—
comprising twenty-eight ice fields from fifty to five-hundred feet
                                                                        thick,
of unimagined delicacy.
"Picking periwinkles from the cracks"
or killing prey with the concentric crushing rigor of the python,
it hovers forward "spider fashion
on its arms" misleadingly like lace;
its "ghostly pallor changing
to the green metallic tinge of an anemone-starred pool."
The fir trees, in "the magnitude of their root systems,"
rise aloof from these maneuvers "creepy to behold,"
austere specimens of our American royal families,
"each like the shadow of the one beside it.
The rock seems frail compared with their dark energy of life,"
its vermilion and onyx and manganese-blue interior expensiveness
left at the mercy of the weather;
"stained transversely by iron where the water drips down,"
recognized by its plants and its animals.
Completing a circle,
you have been deceived into thinking that you have progressed,
under the polite needles of the larches
"hung to filter, not to intercept the sunlight"—
met by tightly wattled spruce twigs
"conformed to an edge like clipped cypress
as if no branch could penetrate the cold beyond its company";
and dumps of gold and silver ore enclosing The Goat's Mirror—
that ladyfinger-like depression in the shape of the left human foot,
which prejudices you in favor of itself
before you have had time to see the others;
its indigo, pea-green, blue-green, and turquoise,
from a hundred to two hundred feet deep,
"merging in irregular patches in the middle lake

where, like gusts of a storm
obliterating the shadows of the fir trees, the wind makes lanes of
ripples."

What spot could have merits of equal importance
for bears, elk, deer, wolves, goats, and ducks?
Pre-empted by their ancestors,
this is the property of the exacting porcupine,
and of the rat "slipping along to its burrow in the swamp
or pausing on high ground to smell the heather";
of "thoughtful beavers
making drains which seem the work of careful men with shovels,"
and of the bears inspecting unexpectedly
ant-hills and berry bushes.
Composed of calcium gems and alabaster pillars,
topaz, tourmaline crystals and amethyst quartz,
their den is somewhere else, concealed in the confusion
of "blue forests thrown together with marble and jasper and agate
as if whole quarries had been dynamited."
And farther up, in stag-at-bay position
as a scintillating fragment of these terrible stalagmites,
stands the goat,
its eye fixed on the waterfall which never seems to fall—
an endless skein swayed by the wind,
immune to force of gravity in the perspective of the peaks.
A special antelope
acclimated to "grottoes from which issue penetrating draughts
which make you wonder why you came,"
it stands its ground
on cliffs the color of the clouds, of petrified white vapor—
black feet, eyes, nose, and horns, engraved on dazzling ice fields,
the ermine body on the crystal peak;
the sun kindling its shoulders to maximum heat like acetylene, dyeing
them white—
upon this antique pedestal,
"a mountain with those graceful lines which prove it a volcano,"
its top a complete cone like Fujiyama's
till an explosion blew it off.
Distinguished by a beauty

of which "the visitor dare never fully speak at home
for fear of being stoned as an impostor,"
Big Snow Mountain is the home of a diversity of creatures:
those who "have lived in hotels
but who now live in camps—who prefer to";
the mountain guide evolving from the trapper,
"in two pairs of trousers, the outer one older,
wearing slowly away from the feet to the knees";
"the nine-striped chipmunk
running with unmammal-like agility along a log";
the water ouzel
with "its passion for rapids and high-pressured falls,"
building under the arch of some tiny Niagara;
the white-tailed ptarmigan "in winter solid white,
feeding on heather-bells and alpine buckwheat";
and the eleven eagles of the west,
"fond of the spring fragrance and the winter colors,"
used to the unegoistic action of the glaciers
and "several hours of frost every midsummer night."
"They make a nice appearance, don't they,"
happy seeing nothing?
Perched on treacherous lava and pumice—
those unadjusted chimney pots and cleavers
which stipulate "names and addresses of persons to notify
in case of disaster"—
they hear the roar of ice and supervise the water
winding slowly through the cliffs,
the road "climbing like the thread
which forms the groove around a snail shell,
doubling back and forth until where snow begins, it ends."
No "deliberate wide-eyed wistfulness" is here
among the boulders sunk in ripples and white water
where "when you hear the best wild music of the forest
it is sure to be a marmot,"
the victim on some slight observatory,
of "a struggle between curiosity and caution,"
inquiring what has scared it:
a stone from the moraine descending in leaps,

another marmot, or the spotted ponies with glass eyes,
brought up on frosty grass and flowers
and rapid draughts of ice water.
Instructed none knows how, to climb the mountain,
by businessmen who require for recreation
three hundred and sixty-five holidays in the year,
these conspicuously spotted little horses are peculiar;
hard to discern among the birch trees, ferns, and lily pads,
avalanche lilies, Indian paintbrushes,
bear's ears and kittentails,
and miniature cavalcades of chlorophylless fungi
magnified in profile on the moss-beds like moonstones in the water;
the cavalcade of calico competing
with the original American menagerie of styles
among the white flowers of the rhododendron surmounting rigid
                                                              leaves
upon which moisture works its alchemy,
transmuting verdure into onyx.

"Like happy souls in Hell," enjoying mental difficulties,
the Greeks
amused themselves with delicate behavior
because it was "so noble and so fair";
not practised in adapting their intelligence
to eagle traps and snowshoes,
to alpenstocks and other toys contrived by those
"alive to the advantage of invigorating pleasures."
Bows, arrows, oars, and paddles, for which trees provide the wood,
in new countries more eloquent than elsewhere—
augmenting the assertion that, essentially humane,
"the forest affords wood for dwellings and by its beauty
stimulates the moral vigor of its citizens."
The Greek liked smoothness, distrusting what was back
of what could not be clearly seen,
resolving with benevolent conclusiveness,
"complexities which still will be complexities
as long as the world lasts";
ascribing what we clumsily call happiness,

to "an accident or a quality,
a spiritual substance or the soul itself,
an act, a disposition, or a habit,
or a habit infused, to which the soul has been persuaded,
or something distinct from a habit, a power"—
such power as Adam had and we are still devoid of.
"Emotionally sensitive, their hearts were hard";
their wisdom was remote
from that of these odd oracles of cool official sarcasm,
upon this game preserve
where "guns, nets, seines, traps and explosives,
hired vehicles, gambling and intoxicants are prohibited;
disobedient persons being summarily removed
and not allowed to return without permission in writing."
It is self-evident
that it is frightful to have everything afraid of one;
that one must do as one is told
and eat rice, prunes, dates, raisins, hardtack, and tomatoes
if one would "conquer the main peak of Mount Tacoma,
this fossil flower concise without a shiver,
intact when it is cut,
damned for its sacrosanct remoteness—
like Henry James "damned by the public for decorum";
not decorum, but restraint;
it is the love of doing hard things
that rebuffed and wore them out—a public out of sympathy with
neatness.

Neatness of finish! Neatness of finish!
Relentless accuracy is the nature of this octopus
with its capacity for fact.
"Creeping slowly as with meditated stealth,
its arms seeming to approach from all directions,"
it receives one under winds that "tear the snow to bits
and hurl it like a sandblast
shearing off twigs and loose bark from the trees."
Is "tree" the word for these things
"flat on the ground like vines"?
some "bent in a half circle with branches on one side

suggesting dust-brushes, not trees;
some finding strength in union, forming little stunted groves
their flattened mats of branches shrunk in trying to escape"
from the hard mountain "planed by ice and polished by the wind"—
the white volcano with no weather side;
the lightning flashing at its base,
rain falling in the valleys, and snow falling on the peak—
the glassy octopus symmetrically pointed,
its claw cut by the avalanche
"with a sound like the crack of a rifle,
in a curtain of powdered snow launched like a waterfall."

Ezra Pound

Born 1885 in Hailey, Idaho. Died 1972 in Italy. On the way from conventional to modern modes before then, his breakthrough into "imagism(e)" came in 1912, cut almost out of whole cloth & still restrained by classicist notions of *good* writing, etc., but produced the influential three dicta: "1. Direct treatment of the 'thing' whether subjective or objective; 2. To use absolutely no word that does not contribute to the presentation; 3. As regarding rhythm: to compose in the sequence of the musical phrase, not in the sequence of the metronome." By 1914 the association with Wyndham Lewis (two issues of *Blast*, etc.) & a strong whiff of Futurism & Cubism brought the earlier definition of "image" ("that which presents an 'intellectual' complex in an instant of time") into the high energy of vorticist theory & the onset of the *Cantos.* The poem appeared in history, in time; the image became a "moving image"; both image & cubist collage were subsumed (along with translation & tradition = "make it new") under the proposition of mind as a vortex, where "all times are contemporaneous," & the poem as a "knot of patterned energies" (H. Kenner) & a process of letting it cohere. While Pound was probably never out of conflict with himself about the (literary) consequences of such a vision, he has continued to influence large areas of contemporary poetry, not only as a poet (*Lustra, Hugh Selwyn Mauberley, Personae,* & the life/time process of *The Cantos*), but as a germinal & experimental translator (*Cathay, Sextus Propertius, Women of Trachis,* etc.), as an editor (*Little Review, Exile, Profile* & *Active Anthologies,* T. S. Elliot's *Waste Land*), & as a man mediating poetics & history in voluminous letters & essays.

" O bright
" Swallow with a white
" Belly and black back,"
etc.

DOGMATIC STATEMENT ON THE GAME AND PLAY OF CHESS.

(THEME FOR A SERIES OF PICTURES).

Red knights, brown bishops, bright queens
Striking the board, falling in strong " L's " of colour,
Reaching and striking in angles,
                    Holding lines of one colour :
This board is alive with light
These pieces are living in form,
         Their moves break and reform the pattern :
Luminous green from the rooks,
         Clashing with " x's " of queens,
                Looped with the knight-leaps.
" Y " pawns, cleaving, embanking,
Whirl, centripetal, mate, King down in the vortex :
Clash, leaping of bands, straight strips of hard colour,
Blocked lights working in, escapes, renewing of contes

VORTEX.

POUND.

The vortex is the point of maximum energy,

It represents, in mechanics, the greatest efficiency.

We use the words " greatest efficiency " in the precise sense—as they would be used in a text book of MECHANICS.

You may think of man as that toward which perception moves. You may think of him as the TOY of circumstance, as the plastic substance RECEIVING impressions.

OR you may think of him as DIRECTING a certain fluid force against circumstance, as CONCEIVING instead of merely observing and reflecting.

THE PRIMARY PIGMENT.

The vorticist relies on this alone ; on the primary pigment of his art, nothing else.

Every conception, every emotion presents itself to the vivid consciousness in some primary form.

It is the picture that means a hundred poems, the music that means a hundred pictures, the most highly energized statement, the statement that has not yet SPENT itself it expression, but which is the most capable of expressing.

THE TURBINE.

All experience rushes into this vortex. All the energized past, all the past that is living and worthy to live. All MOMENTUM, which is the past bearing upon us, RACE, RACE-MEMORY, instinct charging the PLACID,
NON-ENERGIZED FUTURE.

The DESIGN of the future in the grip of the human vortex. All the past that is vital, all the past that is capable of living into the future, is pregnant in the vortex, NOW.

Hedonism is the vacant place of a vortex, without force, deprived of past and of future, the vertex of a stil spool or cone.

Futurism is the disgorging spray of a vortex with no drive behind it, DISPERSAL.

EVERY CONCEPT, EVERY EMOTION PRESENTS ITSELF TO THE VIVID CONSCIOUSNESS IN SOME PRIMARY FORM. IT BELONGS TO THE ART OF THIS FORM. IF SOUND, TO MUSIC ; IF FORMED WORDS, TO LITERATURE ; THE IMAGE, TO POETRY ; FORM, TO DESIGN ; COLOUR IN POSITION, TO PAINTING ; FORM OR DESIGN IN THREE PLANES, to SCULPTURE ; MOVEMENT TO THE DANCE OR TO THE RHYTHM OF MUSIC OR OF VERSES.

Elaboration, expression of second intensities, of dispersedness belong to the secondary sort of artist. Dispersed arts HAD a vortex.

Impressionism, Futurism, which is only an accelerated sort of impressionism, DENY the vortex. They are the CORPSES of VORTICES. POPULAR BELIEFS, movements, etc., are the CORPSES OF VORTICES. Marinetti is a corpse.

THE MAN.

The vorticist relies not upon similarity or analogy, not upon likeness or mimcry.

In painting he does not rely upon the likeness to a beloved grandmother or to a caressable mistress.

VORTICISM is art before it has spread itself into a state of flacidity, of elaboration, of secondary applications.

ANCESTRY.

" All arts approach the conditions of music."—*Pater*.

" An Image is that which presents an intellectual and emotional complex in an instant of time."—*Pound*.

" You are interested in a certain painting because it is an arrangement of lines and colours."—*Whistler*.

Picasso, Kandinski, father and mother, classicism and romanticism of the movement.

POETRY.

The vorticist will use only the primary media of his art.

The primary pigment of poetry is the IMAGE.

The vorticist will not allow the primary expression of any concept or emotion to drag itself out into mimicry.

In painting Kandinski, Picasso.

In poetry this by, " H. D."

> Whirl up sea ——
> Whirl your pointed pines,
> Splash your great pines
> On our rocks,
> Hurl your green over us,
> Cover us with your pools of fir.

CANTO XXXIX

Desolate is the roof where the cat sat,
Desolate is the iron rail that he walked
And the corner post whence he greeted the sunrise.
In hill path: "thkk, thgk"
                    of the loom
" Thgk, thkk " and the sharp sound of a song
            under olives
When I lay in the ingle of Circe
I heard a song of that kind.
            Fat panther lay by me
Girls talked there of fucking, beasts talked there of eating,
All heavy with sleep, fucked girls and fat leopards,
Lions loggy with Circe's tisane,
Girls leery with Circe's tisane
        κακὰ φάρμακ' ἔδοκεν
        kaka pharmak edōken
The house of smooth stone that you can see from a distance
λύκοι ὀρέστεροι, ἠδὲ λέοντες
lukoi oresteroi ede leontes
            wolf to curry favour for food
—born to Helios and Perseis
        That had Pasiphae for a twin
Venter venustus, cunni cultrix, of the velvet marge
            ver novum, canorum, ver novum
Spring overborne into summer
            late spring in the leafy autumn
καλὸν ἀοιδιάει
KALON AOIDIAEI
        'Η θεὸς, ἠὲ γυνή.....φθεγγώμεθα θᾶσσον
        e theos e guné....ptheggometha thasson
First honey and cheese
            honey at first and then acorns
Honey at the start and then acorns
honey and wine and then acorns
Song sharp at the edge, her crotch like a young sapling
illa dolore obmutuit, pariter vocem

’ Ἀλλ’ ἄλλην χρὴ πρῶτον ʽοδὸν τελέσαι, καὶ ʽικεσθαι
Εἰς Ἀΐδαο δόμομς και επαινῆς Περσεφονείης’
Ψυχῆ χρησομένους Οηβαίου Τειρεσίαο
Μάντιος Ἀλαὖν του τε φρένες ἔμπεδοι εἰσι
Τῷ καὶ τεθνηιῶτι νόον πόρε Περσεφόνεια

When Hathor was bound in that box
        afloat on the sea wave
Came Mava swimming with light hand lifted in overstroke
sea blossom wreathed in her locks,
" What are you box? "
        " I am Hathor."
Che mai da me non si parte il diletto
Fulvida di folgore
Came here with Glaucus unnoticed, nec ivi in harum
Nec in harum ingressus sum.
        Discuss this in bed said the lady
Euné kai philoteti ephata Kirke
Εὐνῆ καὶ φιλότητι, ἔφατα Κίρκη
es thalamon
Ἐς θάλαμόν
Eurilochus, Macer, better there with good acorns
Than with a crab for an eye, and 30 fathom of fishes
Green swish in the socket,
        Under the portico Kirké:......
" I think you must be Odysseus....
        feel better when you have eaten....
Always with your mind on the past....
Ad Orcum autem quisquam?
        nondum nave nigra pervenit.....
Been to hell in a boat yet?

Sumus in fide
Puellaeque canamus
sub nocte....
        there in the glade

To Flora's night, with hyacinthus,
With the crocus (spring
                sharp in the grass,)
Fifty and forty together
                ERI MEN AI DE KUDONIAI
Betuene Aprile and Merche
                with sap new in the bough
With plum flowers above them
                with almond on the black bough
With jasmine and olive leaf,
To the beat of the measure
From star up to the half-dark
From half-dark to half-dark
                Unceasing the measure
Flank by flank on the headland
                with the Goddess' eyes to seaward
By Circeo, by Terracina, with the stone eyes
                white toward the sea
With one measure, unceasing:
                " Fac deum! " " Est factus."
Ver novum!
                ver novum!
Thus made the spring,
Can see but their eyes in the dark
                not the bough that he walked on.
Beaten from flesh into light
Hath swallowed the fire-ball
A traverso le foglie
His rod hath made god in my belly
                Sic loquitur nupta
                Cantat sic nupta

Dark shoulders have stirred the lightning
A girl's arms have nested the fire,
Not I but the handmaid kindled
                Cantat sic nupta
I have eaten the flame.

Note. Pound writes in a letter to William Carlos Williams (22 Marzo 1931): "glad to get someone to state that IF they don't understand the greek etc etc.etc. let 'em GO ON, and they will find that they have been told just the same without readink the greek." In other words, if the present editor may offer his extension of said matter: the crux, as with most art & music using "collage," is the **presence** of the collaged elements (for eye & ear)—the reader's recognition of source a variable not imposed but dependent on his own experience. In the case above, most of the Greek involves description of animals & sex, etc., in the Circe section of the **Odyssey**, & the clips of old language constitute another act within the poem, which has elsewhere disclosed its "meaning"; i.e., in Williams' paraphrase of same: "Suddenly . . . there is disclosed an unfamiliar magnificence of fornication—the official sin of constituted stupidity. That sex will be accomplished in sin, is the blind behind which venality has worked to undo the world. Kids may go masturbating into asylums but profits must be preserved. . . . Love versus usury, the living hell-stink of today: time-fuses sold in Germany to blow Germans into manure, French cannon to Turkey to blast Frenchmen to scrapple—the Napoleons, the Krupps—Love on a cliff overlooking the sea, an ecstasy."

Carl Sandburg

Born 1878 in Galesburg, Illinois. Died 1967. He's still probably the most interesting of the populist midwest poets & of that whole off-shoot of early American modernism. The impact, if indirectly, was felt again in the 50s & 60s, & at least one mode deserves re-viewing: his extension of the Whitman "catalogue" to create a poem whose statement rests in the sheer juxtaposition of data, giving the sense (however deceptive) of a compendium devoid of transformations. The other inadvertent triumph of his work is that the language, which may have set out to be *simply* real, now takes on a patina, a kind of funky brightness with half a century between. And Williams' very harsh & very fair assessment of Sandburg's "formlessness" may read differently in an age that has abandoned the perfect & tasteful, to re-explore the possibilities of the aimless & random, etc.: "It is the very formlessness of the material, its failure to affirm anything formal, the drift of aimless life through the six hundred and seventy-six pages that is the form. It had to be shapeless to affirm what was being said: persistence in change." (W. C. W., 1948) Sandburg's early poems (*Chicago Poems, Cornhuskers, Smoke & Steel, Slabs of the Sunburnt West, Good Morning America,* & *The People, Yes*) come together in his *Collected Poems.*

From THE PEOPLE, YES (NO. 53)

> Come on, superstition, and get my goat.
> I got mascots.
> The stars of my birthday favor me.
> The numbers from one to ten are with me.
> I was born under a lucky star and nothing can stop me.

The moon was a waxing moon and not a waning moon when I was
     born.
Every card in the deck and both of the seven-eleven bones are with
     me.
So you hear them tell it and they mean if it works it's good and if it
     don't it costs nothing.
How to win love, how to win games, the spells and conjurations are
     named for fever, burns, convulsions, snakebite, milksick, balk-
     ing horses, rheumatism, warts.
"Tie the heart of a bat with a red silk string to your right arm and
     you will win every game at which you play."
If your right foot itches you will soon start on a journey, if it's your
     left foot you will go where you are not wanted.
If you sing before breakfast you will cry before night, if you sneeze
     before breakfast you will see your true love before Saturday
     night.
Lightning in the north means rain, lightning in the south means dry
     weather.
Frost three months after the first katydid is heard. Three white frosts
     and then a rain.

For toothache the faith doctor wrote the words "galla gaffa gassa"
on the wall. With a nail he pointed at each letter of the words, ask-
ing if the toothache was better. At the letter where the tooth was
feeling easier he drove the nail in and the tooth stopped aching. Galla
gaffa gassa.
Gassa galla gaffa.

> Goofer dust comes from the goofer tree.
> Sprinkle it in the shoes of the woman you love and
>   she can never get away from you.
>   Galla gaffa gassa.

> Even a lousy cur has his lucky days.
> Sweep dirt out of the door after night and
>   you sweep yourself out of a home.
> Shake the tablecloth out of doors after sunset
>   and you will never marry.

The first to drive a hearse is the next to die.
Kill cats, dogs or frogs and you die in rags.
Point at a shooting star or even speak of it and
     you lose your next wish.
Better born lucky than rich.
Marry in May, repent always.
May is the month to marry bad wives.

The son of the white hen brings luck.
So does a horse with four white feet.

He planted gravel and up came potatoes.
When a bitch litters pigs that is luck.
The lucky fellow gets eggs from his rooster
     and his hen eggs have two yolks.
Luck for the few, death for the many.

Ladders of luck, let us
climb your yellow rungs.
Ropes of the up-and-up
send us silver sky-hooks.
Black horses, let us saddle
you with silk belly-bands.
Black cats with orange spots
bring us big ships loaded
with wild Spanish women.
Galloping cubes of fate
hand us sevens elevens
hand us the pretty numbers.
Black moonlight, let a little
of that old gold drop down.
     Black roses? Yes
there must be cool black roses.
Out of the deep night came to us all
     the kiss of the black rose.

Gertrude Stein

Born 1874 in Allegheny, Pennsylvania. Died 1946. Her own appraisal of her work ("the most serious thinking about the nature of literature in the 20th century has been done by a woman") seems reasonable enough compared to the neglect of that work, but particularly the poetry, in established literary circles. She came early to a root investigation of language & form ("going systematically to work smashing every connotation that words ever had, in order to get them back clean"—W. C. W.) & to a poetry that brought "cubism" into language (here as an altered concept of time, the "continuous present") & otherwise set the stage for much that was to follow. Her materials were simple enough to be easily misunderstood, & her declared intention was to "work in the excitedness of pure being . . . To get back that intensity into the language." She could produce work that was literally abstract, the end of a process of experiment by subtraction; or, as she would write later when looking back at *Tender Buttons*: "It was my first conscious struggle with the problem of correlating sight, sound and sense, and eliminating rhythm—now I am trying grammar and eliminating sight and sound" (*Transition* No. 14, Fall, 1928). And it was, at the same time, a struggle to reorder thought & to explore what her teacher, William James, called "other forms of consciousness"—that process recognized in 1913 by Mabel Dodge, who wrote in the special issue of Stieglitz's *Camera Work*: "Nearly every thinking person nowadays is in revolt against something, because the craving of the individual is for further consciousness and because consciousness is expanding and is bursting through the moulds that have held it up to now. And so let every man whose private truth is too great for his existing conditions pause before he turn away from Picasso's painting or from Gertrude Stein's writing, for their case is his case." Only over the last few years has this become clear again, with the reissuing (in a poetry context) of certain key works: *Geography & Plays, As a Wife Has a Cow,* & *Matisse, Picasso & Gertrude Stein* by Something Else Press, & *How Writing Is Written* & *Primer for the Gradual Understanding of Gertrude Stein* by Black Sparrow. Along with the nearly unavailable Yale series (*Bee Time Vine, Alphabets & Birthdays, Painted Lace,* & *Stanzas in Meditation*) & other collections that largely draw on her prose work, these form an extraordinary cross-section from an endlessly variable series of experiments in poesis & meditation.

Now to come back to how I know what I know about poetry.

I was writing The Making of Americans, *I was completely obsessed by the inner life of everything including generations of everybody's living and I was writing prose, prose that had to do with the balancing the inner balancing of everything. I have already told you all about that.*

And then, something happened and I began to discover the names of things, that is not discover the names but discover the things the things to see the things to look at and in so doing I had of course to name them not to give them new names but to see that I could find out how to know that they were there by their names or by replacing their names. And how was I to do so. They had their names and naturally I called them by the names they had and in doing so having begun looking at them I called them by their names with passion and that made poetry, I did not mean it to make poetry but it did, it made the Tender Buttons, *and the* Tender Buttons *was very good poetry it made a lot more poetry, and I will now more and more tell about that and how it happened.*

*

From TENDER BUTTONS

A DOG

A little monkey goes like a donkey that means to say that means to say that more sighs last goes. Leave with it. A little monkey goes like a donkey.

A WHITE HUNTER

A white hunter is nearly crazy.

A LEAVE

In the middle of a tiny spot and nearly bare there is a nice thing to say that wrist is leading. Wrist is leading.

SUPPOSE AN EYES

Suppose it is within a gate which open is open at the hour of closing summer that is to say so.

All the seats are needing blackening. A white dress is in sign. A soldier a real soldier has a worn lace a worn lace of different sizes that is to say if he can read, if he can read he is a size to show shutting up twenty-four.

Go red go red, laugh white.

Suppose a collapse in rubbed purr, in rubbed purr get.

Little sales ladies little sales ladies little saddles of mutton.

Little sales of leather and such beautiful beautiful, beautiful beautiful.

*

You see what I mean, I did express what something was, a little by talking and listening to that thing, but a great deal by looking at that thing.

This as I say has been the great problem of our generation, so much happens and anybody at any moment knows everything that is happening that things happening although interesting are not really exciting. And an artist an artist inevitably has to do what is really exciting. That is what he is inside him, that is what an artist really is inside him, he is exciting, and if he is not there is nothing to any of it.

A CURTAIN RAISER

Six.
Twenty.
                   Outrageous.
Late,
Weak.
                       Forty.
More in any wetness.
Sixty three certainly.
Five.
Sixteen.
Seven.
Three.
More in orderly. Seventy-five.

THEY MAY BE SAID TO BE READY

I
More than they liked.
More than they liked. Them.

II
For it. To be. At last. Lost.

III
Which they made ready. For them.

IV
They were waiting. For them.
They were ready when. They were waiting. Then. For them.

V
More often they were ready.
With them.
Especially. With them.

VI
It is a pleasure. For them.
To be ready. With them.

As much as they can. Be ready. With them.

It is very strange. That when summer begins. They are not ready. For them.

Because during the winter. They are busy. Occupying themselves. With them.

Mine. One. At a time.

It is very ready. To be ready. With them.
Are you ready.

For them. Or. With them.

Many. Are ready. For them.

BEFORE THE FLOWERS OF FRIENDSHIP FADED FRIENDSHIP FADED

Written on a poem by Georges Hugnet

In the one hundred small places of myself my youth,
And myself in if it is the use of passion,
In this in it and in the nights alone
If in the next to night which is indeed not well
I follow you without it having slept and went.
Without the pressure of a place with which to come unfolded folds
    are a pressure and an abusive stain
A head if uncovered can be as hot, as heated,
to please to take a distance to make life,
And if resisting, little, they have no thought,
a little one which was a little which was as all as still,
Or with or without fear or with it all,
And if in feeling all it will be placed alone beside
And it is with with which and not beside not beside may,

Outside with much which is without with me, and not an Indian
    shawl, which could it be but with my blood.

II
A little a little one all wooly or in wool
As if within or not in any week or as for weeks
A little one which makes a street no name
without it having come and went farewell
And not with laughing playing
Where they went they would or work
it is not that they look alike with which in up and down as chickens
    without dogs,
Coming to have no liking for a thief which is not left to have away,
To live like when
And very many things
Being with me with them with which with me whoever with and
    born and went as well
Meant,
Five which are seen
And with it five more lent,
As much as not mixed up,
With love

III
I often live with many months with years of which I think
And they as naturally think well of those
My littlest shoes which were not very much without that care left
    there
where I would like the heat
and very nearly find that trees have many little places that make shade
Which never went away when there was sun
In a way there were cries and it was felt to be the cruelest yet
I am very happy in my play
and I am very thirsty in hunger
Which is not what is always there with love
And after all when was I born.
I can touch wood and think
I can also see girls who were in finding
and they will laugh and say

And yes say so as yes as yes with woe
And now they with me think and love love that they hold with hide
    and even
It is as if all fields would grow what do they grow, tobacco even so,
And they will not delight in having had,
Because after no fear and not afraid,
they have been having that they join as well,
And always it is pretty to see dogs.
It is no double to have more with when they met and in began who
    can.
There is very little to hide,
When there is everything beside
And there is a well inside
In hands untied.

IV
I follow as I can and this to do
With never vaguely that they went away
I have been left to bargain with myself
And I have come not to be pleased to see
They wish to watch the little bird
Who flew at which they look
They never mentioned me to it,
I stopped to listen well it is a pleasure to see a fire which does not
    inspire them to see me
I wish to look at dogs
Because they will be having with they wish
To have it look alike as when it does.

V
Everything is best of all for you which is for me,
I like a half of which it is as much
Which never in alone is more than most
Because I easily can be repaid in difficulty of the hurry left
Between now not at all and after which began
It could be morning which it was at night
And little things do feed a little more than all
What was it that was meant by things as said
There is a difference between yet and well

And very well and when there was as much which is as well as more
And it is very likely made away again
Very nearly as much as not before
Which is as better than to have it now
Which it is taken to make my blood thin.

VI
It is very likely counting it as well
Named not alas but they must lend it for
In welcome doubt which they need for deceit
They face a little more than most and made it.
They will be born in better than at least with not at all relieved and
    left away a little said
Which is not with made not unless.
Unless is used with where liked what.

VII
A very long a little way
They have to have
In which array
They make it wring
Their tendering them this.
It is whatever originally read read can be two words smoke can be
    all three
And very much there were.
It is larger than around to think them a little amiably
What is it said to incline learnt and places it as place
As which were more than the two made it do.
Remember not a color
Every little boy has his own desk.

VIII
Who leaves it to be left to like it less
which is to leave alone what they have left
They made it act as if to shout
Is when they make it come away and sit.
Nobody need say no nor yes.
They who had known or which was pressed as press
They might with thought come yet to think without
With which it is to like it with its shell,

A shell has hold of what is not with held
It is just as well not to be well as well
Nevertheless
As when it is in short and long and pleasure
It is a little thing to ask to wait
It is in any kind of many chances
They like it best with all its under weight
And will they miss it when they meet its frame,
A frame is such that hours are made by sitting
Rest it in little pieces
He says we say she says
When it is very well it is not more than still it is not more than ill
And all he says it is and all and very well and very much that was of
    very ill.
And anyway who was as strong as very strong with all and come
    along,
It is a height which makes it best to come to be a matter that they had
Alike in not no end of very well and in divide with better than the
    most,
And very well who knows of very well and best and most and not as
    well as ill.
It could be made as curly as they lie which when they think with me.
Who is with me that is not why they went to be just now.
Just now can be well said.
In imitation there is no more sign than If I had not been without my
    filling it with absence made in choosing extra bright.
I do mind him, I do mind them I do mind her,
Which was the same as made it best for me for her for them.
Any leaf is more annoying than a tree when this you see see me she
    said of me of three of two of me.
And then I went to think of me of which of one of two of one of
    three of which of me I went to be away of three of two of one
    of me.
Any pleasure leads to me and I lead them away away from pleasure
    and from me.

XII
I am very hungry when I drink
I need to leave it when I have it held,

They will be white with which they know they see, that darker makes it be a color white for me, white is not shown when I am dark indeed with red despair who comes who has to care that they will let me a little lie like now I like to lie I like to live I like to die I like to lie and live and die and live and die and by and by I like to live and die and by and by they need to sew, the difference is that sewing makes it bleed and such with them in all the way of seed and seeding and repine and they will which is mine and not all mine who can be thought curious of this of all of that made it and come lead it and done weigh it and mourn and sit upon it know it for ripeness without deserting all of it of which without which it has not been born. Oh no not to be thirsty with the thirst of hunger not alone to know that they plainly and ate or wishes. Any little one will kill himself for milk.

XIII

Known or not known to follow or not follow or not lead.
It is all oak when known as not a tree,
It is all best of all as well as always gone when always sent
In all a lent for all when grass is dried and grass can dry when all
    have gone away and come back then to stay.
Who might it be that they can see that candied is a brush that
    bothers me.
Any way come any way go any way stay any way show any way
    show me.
They ask are peas in one beets in another one beans in another one,
They follow yes beets are in one peas are in one beans are in one.
They hear without a letter which they love, they love above they
    sit and when they sit they stare.
So when a little one has more and any one has more and who has
    more who has more when there can be heard enough and not
    enough of where.
Who has more where.

XIV

It could be seen very nicely
That doves have each a heart,
Each one is always seeing that they could not be apart,
A little lake makes fountains
And fountains have no flow,

And a dove has need of flying
And water can be low,
Let me go.
Any week is what they seek
When they have to halve a beak.
I like a painting on a wall of doves
And what do they do,
They have hearts
They are apart
Little doves are winsome
But not when they are little and left.

XV

It is always just as well
That there is a better bell
Than that with which a half is a whole
Than that with which a south is a pole
Than that with which they went away to stay
Than that with which after any way,
Needed to be gay to-day.

XVI

Any little while is longer any little while is shorter any little
while is better any little while for me when this you see then think
of me.

It is very sad that it is very bad that badly and sadly and mourn
and shorn and torn and thorn and best and most and at least and all
and better than to call if you call you sleep and if you sleep you must
and if you must you shall and if you shall when then when is it then
that Angelina she can see it make it be that it is all that it can have it
color color white white is for black what green which is a hope is
for a yellow which can be very sweet and it is likely that a long
tender not as much as most need names to make a cake or dance or
loss or next or sweetening without sugar in a cell or most unlikely
with it privately who makes it be called practice that they came.
They come thank you they come. Any little grass is famous to be
grass grass green and red blue and all out but you.

XVII

He is the exact age he tells you

He is not twenty two, he is twenty three and when this you see
 remember me,
And yet what is it that he can see,
He can see veritably three, all three which is to be certainly
And then.

He tells of oceans which are there and little lakes as well he sings
it lightly with his voice and thinks he had to shout and not at all
with oceans near and not at all at all, he thinks he is he will he does
he knows he was he knows he was he will he has he is he does and
now and when is it to be to settle without sillily to be without with-
out with doubt let me. So he says. It is easy to put heads together
really. Head to head it is easily done and easily said head to head
in bed.

XVIII
When I sleep I sleep and do not dream because it is as well that I
 am what I seem when I am in my bed and dream.

XIX
It was with him that he was little tall and old and just as young
as when begun by seeming soldiers young and hold and with a little
change in place who hopes that women are a race will they be thin
will they like fat does milk does hope does age does that no one can
think when all have thought that they will think but have not
bought no without oceans who hears wheat do they like fish think
well of meat it is without without a change that they like this they
have it here it is with much that left by him he is within within
within actually how many hear actually what age is here actually
they are with hope actually they might be bespoke believe me it is
not for pleasure that I do it. They often have too much rain as well
as too much sun.
They will not be won.
One might be one.
Might one be one.

XX
A little house is always held
By a little ball which is always held,
By a little hay which is always held
By a little house which is always held,

A house and a tree a little house and a large tree,
And a little house not for them and a large tree.
And after all fifteen are older that one two three.

It is useful that no one is barred from looking out of a house to see a tree even when there is a tree to see. She made it mentioned when she was not there and so was he.

XXI

He likes that felt is made of beaver and cotton made of trees and feathers made of birds and red as well. He likes it.

XXII

He likes to be with her so he says does he like to be with her so he says.

XXIII

Every one which is why they will they will be will he will he be for her for her to come with him with when he went he went and came and any little name is shame as such tattoo. Any little ball is made a net and any little net is made for mine and any little mine that any have will always violate the hope of this which they wore as they lose. It is a welcome, nobody knows a circumstance is with whatever water wishes now. It is pleasant that without a hose no water is drawn. No water is drawn pleasantly without a hose. Doublet and hose not at all water and hose not at all any not at all. Not at all. Either not at all by not at all with me. When this you do not hear and do not see believe me.

XXIV

They were easily left alone they were as easily left alone they were as easily left alone with them. Which makes mistakes mistakes which are mistakes who mistakes mistakes let them see the seal what is the difference between seal and school what is the difference between school and singing school and seeing school and leaving school and sitting in a school. They know the difference when they see the screen which is why leaves are dry when rain is thin and appetising which can be when they win. They win a little exercise in win. Win and win. Perhaps with happens to be thin. It is not easy to be led by them. Not easy to be led and led and led to no brim. In doubt not with them. Not in doubt not with them. Leave it to me to know three from three and they did leave it to him.

XXV

It is easy to mingle sails with steam oil with coal water with air, it is easy to mingle everywhere and to leave single everywhere water and air oil and coal butter and a share it is a share to ask them where and in a little they will have it there they like it there they had it to prepare and to be a comfort to them without care. It is a need to see without a glare of having it come in does it come in and where. They like a little dog to be afraid to have a nightingale be told a chicken is afraid and it is true he is she is and where whenever there is a hawk up in the air. Like that. It makes anybody think of sail-boats.

XXVI

Little by little two go if two go three go if three go four go if four go they go. It is known as does he go he goes if they go they go and they know they know best and most of whether he will go. He is to go. They will not have vanilla and say so. To go Jenny go, Ivy go Gaby go any come and go is go and come and go and leave to go. Who has to hold it while they go who has to who has had it held and have them come to go. He went and came and had to go. No one has had to say he had to go come here to go go there to go go go to come to come to go to go and come and go.

XXVII

In a little while they smile in a little while and one two three they smile they smile a while in a little while a little smile with which to smile a while and when they like to be as once in a while it is about the time with which in which to smile. He can smile and any smile is when as when to smile. It is to show that now that he can know and if to smile it is to smile and smile that he can know and any making it be ready there for them to see to change a smile to change a smile into a stare and very likely more than if they care he can care does and will and not to have to care and this is made with and without a need to carry horses horses without sails sails have an ocean sometimes just the land but to believe to have relief in them who can share horses sails and little less a very little less and they like them. It does it hope. They come they see they sew and always with it a hope is for more not more than yesterday but more to-day more to-day more to say more to-day. A little long and birds can drink with beaks and chickens do and horses drink and sails and even all.

XXVIII

A clock in the eye ticks in the eye a clock ticks in the eye.

A number with that and large as a hat which makes rims think
    quicker than I.

A clock in the eye ticks in the eye a clock ticks ticks in the eye.

XXIX

I love my love with a v
Because it is like that
I love myself with a b
Because I am beside that
A king.
I love my love with an a
Because she is a queen
I love my love and a a is the best of then
Think well and be a king,
Think more and think again
I love my love with a dress and a hat
I love my love and not with this or with that
I love my love with a y because she is my bride
I love her with a d because she is my love beside
Thank you for being there
Nobody has to care
Thank you for being here
Because you are not there.

    And with and without me which is and without she she can be
late and then and how and all around we think and found that it is
time to cry she and I.

XXX

There are a few here now and the rest can follow a cow,
The rest can follow now there are a few here now,
They are all all here now the rest can follow a cow
And mushrooms on a hill and anything else until
They can see and sink and swim with now and then a brim,
A brim to a hat
What is that,
Anyway in the house they say
Anyway any day
Anyway every day

Anyway outside as they may
Think and swim with hearing him,
Love and sing not any song a song it always then too long to just sit
    there and sing
Sing song is a song
When sing and sung
Is just the same as now among
Among them,
They are very well placed to be seated and sought
They are very well placed to be cheated and bought
And a bouquet makes a woods
A hat makes a man
And any little more is better than
The one.
And so a boat a goat and wood
And so a loaf which is not said to be just bread
Who can be made to think and die
And any one can come and cry and sing.
Which made butter look yellow
And a hope be relieved
By all of it in case
Of my name.
What is my name.
That is the game
Georges Hugnet
By Gertrude Stein.

Note. "Flowers of Friendship" began as Stein's translation of Georges Hugnet's poem, **Enfance**, but after the opening sections, she took off on her own, finding "(the words) went one into the other in a different kind of a fashion than any words ever had done before any words that I had ever written and I was perplexed at what was happening and I finished the whole thing not translating but carrying out an idea which was already existing." Originally published, with accompanying French text, under the title, "Poem Pritten on Pfances of Georges Hugnet," in **Pagany**, Volume II, No. 1 (1931).

From THE MOTHER OF US ALL

We cannot retrace our steps, going forward may be the same as going backwards. We cannot retrace our steps, retrace our steps. All my long life, all my life, we do not retrace our steps, all my long life, but.

(*A silence a long silence*)

But—we do not retrace our steps, all my long life, and here, here we are here, in marble and gold, did I say gold, yes I said gold, in marble and gold and where—

(*A silence*)

Where is where. In my long life of effort and strife, dear life, life is strife, in my long life, it will not come and go, I tell you so, it will stay it will pay but

(*A long silence*)

But do I want what we have got, has it not gone, what made it live, has it not gone because now it is had, in my long life in my long life

(*Silence*)

Life is strife, I was a martyr all my life not to what I won but to what was done.

(*Silence*)

Do you know because I tell you so, or do you know, do you know.

(*Silence*)

My long life, my long life.

Curtain

Wallace Stevens

Born 1879 in Reading, Pennsylvania. Died 1955. He sought, as he said, "the poem of the mind in the act of finding / what will suffice" —or, simply, "the poem of the act of the mind." Although he rarely left conventional forms behind ("it comes to this, I suppose, that I believe in freedom regardless of form"), the process of that mind (= imagination) brought him like Stein with her "continuous present" to what a critic described as "a sense while reading him that creation is proceeding before one's eyes." His poetry, open to what Armand Schwerner calls "the extraordinary reality of being, just being, moving, changing, flowing in the present," approaches &/or surpasses the French & Spanish modernists in its vision of the "surreal" within the "real." But even his criticism of surrealism ("to make a clam play an accordion is to invent not to discover") & his sense of the normality of all that as a different but necessary "miracle of logic" brings him close to the propositions of a number of post-World War II poets, the present editor among them. Or Stevens again:

> . . . to impose is not
> To discover. To discover an order as of
> A season, to discover summer and know it,
>
> To discover winter and know it well, to find
> Not to impose, not to have reasoned at all,
> Out of nothing to have come on major weather,
>
> It is possible, possible, possible. It must
> Be possible. . . .

("Notes Toward a Supreme Fiction")

His poetry travels from the visual & auditory play of *Harmonium* (1923), through *Ideas of Order* (1935), *The Man with the Blue Guitar* (1937), *Parts of a World* (1942), & *Transport to Summer* (1947) to "the shadowy possibilities of a central stasis" (Schwerner) in *The Auroras of Autumn* (1950) & *The Rock*. The available gatherings are *The Collected Poems* (1954) & *Opus Posthumous* (1957).

CONNOISSEUR OF CHAOS

I

A. A violent order is disorder; and
B. A great disorder is an order. These
Two things are one. (Pages of illustrations.)

II

If all the green of spring was blue, and it is;
If the flowers of South Africa were bright
On the tables of Connecticut, and they are;
If Englishmen lived without tea in Ceylon, and they do;
And if it all went on in an orderly way,
And it does; a law of inherent opposites,
Of essential unity, is as pleasant as port,
As pleasant as the brush-strokes of a bough,
An upper, particular bough in, say, Marchand.

III

After all the pretty contrast of life and death
Proves that these opposite things partake of one,
At least that was the theory, when bishops' books
Resolved the world. We cannot go back to that.
The squirming facts exceed the squamous mind,
If one may say so. And yet relation appears,
A small relation expanding like the shade
Of a cloud on sand, a shape on the side of a hill.

A.   Well, an old order is a violent one.
This proves nothing. Just one more truth, one more
Element in the immense disorder of truths.
B.   It is April as I write. The wind
Is blowing after days of constant rain.
All this, of course, will come to summer soon.
But suppose the disorder of truths should ever come
To an order, most Plantagenet, most fixed . . .
A great disorder is an order. Now, A
And B are not like statuary, posed
For a vista in the Louvre. They are things chalked
On the sidewalk so that the pensive man may see.

V

The pensive man . . . He sees that eagle float
For which the intricate Alps are a single nest.

William Carlos Williams

Born 1883 in Rutherford, New Jersey. Died 1963. Of the first generation of dominant American moderns, he was the most open to the full range of new forms & possibilities: to the actual scope of what had to be done. Along with the Pound association—going back to his student days at the University of Pennsylvania—he engaged directly during the First World War with such as the Others group & the N. Y. Dadaists, & wrote of that time: "There had been a break somewhere: we were streaming through, each thinking his own thoughts, driving his own designs toward his self's objectives. Whether the Armory Show in painting did it or whether that also was no more than a facet—the poetic line, the way the image was to lie on the page was our immediate concern. For myself all that implied in the materials, respecting the place I knew best, was finding a local assertion—to my everlasting relief." With Robert McAlmon in the early 1920s he co-edited *Contact* & was later an adviser to Charles Henri Ford's *Blues*, Richard Johns' *Pagany*, &, most significantly, the "Objectivists" group (Zukofsky, Reznikoff, Oppen, *et al.*). His ongoing concerns were with the relation of poetry to the given state of the language & to the details & particulars of experience: the materials *de facto* through which the imagination could act. In the 1950s the pattern of his sympathies—his exploration of a "new measure" & the "poem as a field of action," along with the need to transform the idea of tradition & the social ground of poetry—brought his work to the center of a number of poetic "movements": projectivists, Beats, etc. The present selection focuses on the early 1920s, when Williams was working on the "improvisations" & non-sequential arrangments of *Kora in Hell* & *Spring and All* (below), with its interplay of prose & verse, leading in effect to the concept & structure of *Paterson*, the complex long poem whose appearance was being eagerly awaited by the end of the

Second World War. His other major books between 1917 & 1945 were *Al Que Quiere* (1917), *Sour Grapes* (1921), *Collected Poems* (1934), & *The Wedge* (1944)—gathered 1950/51 in the *Collected Earlier Poems* & the *Collected Later Poems*—plus novels, plays, short stories, & *In the American Grain*, a germinal work toward the redefinition of the American past.

From SPRING AND ALL

IX

What about all this writing ?

O " Kiki "
O Miss Margaret Jarvis
The backhandspring

I : clean
      clean
      clean : yes.. New York
Wrigley's, appendicitis, John Marin :
skyscraper soup —

Either that or a bullet !

Once
anything might have happened
You lay relaxed on my knees —
the starry night
spread out warm and blind
above the hospital —

Pah !

It is unclean
which is not straight to the mark —

In my life the furniture eats me

the chairs, the floor
the walls
which heard your sobs
drank up my emotion —
they which alone know everything

and snitched on us in the morning —

What to want ?

Drunk we go forward surely
Not I

beds, beds, beds
elevators, fruit, night-tables
breasts to see, white and blue —
to hold in the hand, to nozzle

It is not onion soup
Your sobs soaked through the walls
breaking the hospital to pieces

Everything
— windows, chairs
obscenely drunk, spinning —
white, blue, orange
— hot with our passion

wild tears, desperate rejoinders
my legs, turning slowly
end over end in the air !

But what would you have ?

All I said was :
there, you see, it is broken

stockings, shoes, hairpins
your bed, I wrapped myself round you —
I watched.

You sobbed, you beat your pillow
you tore your hair
you dug your nails into your sides

I was your nightgown
      I watched !

Clean is he alone
after whom stream
the broken pieces of the city —
flying apart at his approaches

but I merely
caressed you curiously

fifteen years ago and you still
go about the city, they say
patching up sick school children

  Understood in a practical way, without calling upon mystic agencies, of this or that order, it is that life becomes actual only when it is identified with ourselves. When we name it, life exists. To repeat physical experiences has no —

  The only means he has to give value to life is to recognise it with the imagination and name it ; this is so. To repeat and repeat the thing without naming it is only to dull the sense and results in frustration.

this makes the artist the prey of life. He is easy of attack.

  I think often of my earlier work and what it has cost me not to have been clear. I acknowledge I have moved chaotically about refusing or rejecting most things, seldom accepting values or acknowledging anything.

        because I early recognised the futility of acquisitive understanding and at the same time rejected religious dogmatism. My whole life has been spent (so far) in seeking to place a value upon experience and the objects of experience that would satisfy my sense of inclusiveness without redundancy — completeness, lack of frustration with the liberty of choice ; the things which the pursuit of " art " offers —

But though I have felt " free " only in the presence of works of the imagination, knowing the quickening of the sense which came of it, and though this experience has held me firm at such times, yet being of a slow but accurate understanding, I have not always been able to complete the intellectual steps which would make me firm in the position.

So most of my life has been lived in hell — a hell of repression lit by flashes of inspiration, when a poem such as this or that would appear

What would have happened in a world similarly lit by the imagination

Oh yes, you are a writer ! a phrase that has often damned me, to myself. I rejected it with heat but the stigma remained. Not a man, not an understanding but a WRITER. I was unable to recognize.

I do not forget with what heat too I condemned some poems of some contemporary praised because of their loveliness —

I find that I was somewhat mistaken — ungenerous

Life's processes are very simple. One or two moves are made and that is the end. The rest is repetitious.

The Improvisations — coming at a time when I was trying to remain firm at great cost — I had recourse to the expedient of letting life go completely in order to live in the world of my choice.

I let the imagination have its own way to see if it could save itself. Something very definite came of it. I found myself alleviated but most important I began there and then to revalue experience, to understand what I was at —

The virtue of the improvisations is their placement in a world of new values —

their fault is their dislocation of sense, often complete. But it is the best I could do under the circumstances. It was the best I could do and retain any value to experience at all.

Now I have come to a different condition. I find that the values there discovered can be extended. I find myself extending the understanding to the work of others and to other things —

I find that there is work to be done in the creation of new forms, new names for experience

and that " beauty " is related not to " loveliness " but to a state in which reality plays a part

Such painting as that of Juan Gris, coming after the impressionists, the expressionists, Cézanne — and dealing severe strokes as well to the expressionists as to the impressionists group — points forward to what will prove the greatest painting yet produced.

— the illusion once dispensed with, painting has this problem before it : to replace not the forms but the reality of experience with its own —

up to now shapes and meanings but always the illusion relying on composition to give likeness to " nature "

now works of art cannot be left in this category of France's " lie," they must be real, not " realism " but reality itself —

they must give not the sense of frustration but a sense of completion, of actuality — It is not a matter of " representation " — much may be represented actually, but of separate existence.

enlargement — revivification of values,

X

The universality of things
draws me toward the candy
with melon flowers that open

about the edge of refuse
proclaiming without accent
the quality of the farmer's

shoulders and his daughter's
accidental skin, so sweet
with clover and the small

yellow cinquefoil in the
parched places. It is
this that engages the favorable

distortion of eyeglasses
that see everything and remain
related to mathematics —

in the most practical frame of
brown celluloid made to
represent tortoiseshell —

A letter from the man who
wants to start a new magazine
made of linen

and he owns a typewriter —
July 1, 1922
All this is for eyeglasses

to discover. But
they lie there with the gold
earpieces folded down

tranquilly Titicaca —

TWO

Continuities

The mutability of the truth. Ibsen said it. Jefferson said it. We should have a revolution of some sort in America every ten years. The truth has to be re-dressed, re-examined, reaffirmed in a new mode. There has to be new poetry. But the thing is that the change, the greater material, the altered structure of the inevitable revolution must be *in* the poem, in it. Made of it. It must shine in the structural body of it.

—WILLIAM CARLOS WILLIAMS (1939)

Hart Crane

Born 1899 in Garretsville, Ohio. Died 1932. Williams' summary of
their differences ("I suppose the thing was that he was searching
for something inside, while I was all for a sharp use of the materials")
seems retrospectively okay, provided one sees it against the actual
movements of their work & climates of their time. For Crane, the
change of materials *outside* the poem becomes meaningful as the
poet's mind absorbs & redirects it toward a "submission to, and ex-
amination and assimilation of the organic effects on us of these and
other fundamental factors of our experience"; thus

> . . . It is my hope to go *through* the combined materials of the
> poem, using our "real" world somewhat as a springboard and to
> give the poem as a *whole* an orbit or predetermined direction
> of its own . . . not toward decoration or amusement, but rather
> toward a state of consciousness, an "innocence" (Blake) or
> absolute beauty. In this condition there may be discoverable
> under new forms certain spiritual illuminations, shining with a
> morality essentialized from experience directly, and not from
> previous precepts or preconceptions.

But his commitment to the transformative energies of "modern
poetry" (& the possibility too of its generating an epic American
poem) stops short at the inherited boundaries of poetic language, &
his decision to turn back in that sense sets him apart from more
radical poets & explains his relation to the academicizers of the
1930s & 40s. Even so, his use of mixed levels of language, his ex-
tensions of the Rimbaudian prose poem, "the pacing of the rhythm
of [his] lines, the syntax, the intensely human tone, or simply the
punctuation" (R. Creeley), along with his personal/ interiorizing/
"prophetic" stance (visible at a time when other of his contempo-

raries still commited to "rebellion against . . . the so-called classical strictures" had disappeared from view) have kept interest in his work & life continuous over the last two decades. The two major books published during his lifetime were *White Buildings* (1926) & *The Bridge* (1930), & the currently available collection is *The Complete Poems & Selected Letters & Prose.*

Poetic prophecy in the case of the seer has nothing to do with factual prediction or with futurity. It is a peculiar type of perception, capable of apprehending some absolute and timeless concept of imagination with astounding clarity and conviction.
1930

THE MANGO TREE

Let them return, saying you blush again for the great Great-grand-mother. It's all like Christmas.

When you sprouted Paradise a discard of chewing-gum took place. Up jug to musical, hanging jug just gay spiders yoked you first,—silking of shadows good underdrawers for owls.

First-plucked before and since the Flood, old hypnotisms wrench the golden boughs. Leaves spatter dawn from emerald cloud-sprockets. Fat final prophets with lean bandits crouch: and dusk is close
under your noon,
you Sun-heap, whose
ripe apple-lanterns gush history, recondite lightnings, irised.
O mister Señor
missus Miss
Mademoiselle
with baskets
Maggy, come on

Harry Crosby

Born 1898. Died 1929. In the last two years of his life, Crosby had developed into a major image-making poet. The myth he unfolded was of the Sun—both as male & female—& he followed its orders through a striking series of structural innovations. Editor of Black Sun Press in Paris (which published works by Hart Crane, Archibald MacLeish, Eugene Jolas, & D. H. Lawrence, along with his own first books). Crosby's verse experiments included the use of found forms (racing charts, book lists, stock reports, etc.) & concrete poetry, all concerned with sun-related imagery. After his suicide, several volumes appeared, with introductions by Eliot, Lawrence & Pound, among others. But in the anti-"modernist" reaction of the 1930s he was turned into a virtual non-person. In the context of the 1970s the importance of his vision would seem clear—its dimensions suggested in Pound's earlier summary, *viz*: "There is more theology in this book of Crosby's than in all the official ecclesiastical utterance of our generation. Crosby's life was a religious manifestation. His death was, if you like, a comprehensible emotional act. . . . A death from excess vitality. A vote of confidence in the cosmos. . . . Perhaps the best indication one can give of Crosby's capacity as a writer is to say that his work gains by being read all together. I do not mean this as a slight compliment. It is true of a small minority only." The key books, all long out of print, are *Torchbearer*, *Mad Queen*, *Chariot of the Sun*, *Transit of Venus*, *Sleeping Together*, & an autobiography, *Shadows of the Sun*.

In Nine Decades
a Mad Queen shall be born

PHOTOHELIOGRAPH (FOR LADY A.)

black black black black black
black black black black black
black black black black black
black black black black black
black black SUN black black
black black black black black
black black black black black
black black black black black
black black black black black
black black black black black

SHORT INTRODUCTION TO THE WORD

1)

Take the word Sun which burns permanently in my brain. It has accuracy and alacrity. It is monomaniac in its intensity. It is a continual flash of insight. It is the marriage of Invulnerability with Yes, of the Red Wolf with the Gold Bumblebee, of Madness with Ra.

2)

Birdileaves, Goldabbits, Fingertoes, Auroramor, Barbarifire, Parabolaw, Peaglecock, Lovegown, Nombrilomane.

3)

I understand certain words to be single and by themselves and deriving from no other words as for instance the word I.

4)

I believe that certain physical changes in the brain result in a given word—this word having the distinguished characteristic of unreality being born neither as a result of connotation nor of conscious endeavor: Starlash.

5)

There is the automatic word as for instance with me the word Sorceress; when the word goes on even while my attention is focused on entirely different subjects just as in swimming my arms and legs go on automatically even when my attention is focused on subjects entirely different from swimming such as witchcraft for instance or the Sorceress.

TATTOO

I am the criminal whose chest is tattooed with a poinard above which are graven the words "mort aux bourgeois." Let us each tattoo this on our hearts.

I am the soldier with a red mark on my nakedness—when in a frenzy of love the mark expands to spell Mad Queen. Let us each tattoo our Mad Queen on our heart.

I am the prophet from the land of the Sun whose back is tattooed in the design of a rising sun. Let us each tattoo a rising sun on our heart.

PHARMACIE DU SOLEIL

calcium iron hydrogen sodium nickel
magnesium cobalt silicon aluminium
titanium chromium strontium manganese
vanadium barium carbon scandium yttrium
zirconium molybdenum lanthanum niobium
palladium neodymium copper zinc cadmium
cerium glucinum germanium rhodium silver
tin lead erbium potassium iridium
tantalum osmium thorium platinum tungsten
ruthenium uranium.

ACADEMY OF STIMULANTS

Do you know what an explosion is or a madness? Do you know the three great elements in an attack? Do you know the voltage required to create a current between the artery of the heart and the Sun?

MADMAN

When I look into the Sun I sun-lover sun-worshipper sun-seeker when I look into the Sun (sunne sonne soleil sol) what is it in the Sun I deify—

His madness: his incorruptibility: his central intensity and fire: his permanency of heat: his candle-power (fifteen hundred and seventy-five billions—1.575.000.000.000.000.000.000.000.000.): his age and duration: his dangerousness to man as seen by the effects (heat-stroke, insolation, thermic fever, siriasis) he sometimes produces upon the nervous system: the healing virtues of his rays (restores youthful vigor and vitality is the source of health and energy oblivionizes ninety per cent of all human aches and pains): his purity (he can penetrate into unclean places brothels privies prisons and not be polluted by them): his magnitude (400 times as large as the moon): his weight (two octillions of tons or 746 times as heavy as the combined weights of all the planets): his brilliance (5300 times brighter than the dazzling radiance of incandescent metal): his distance from the earth as determined by the equation of light, the constant of abberation, the parallectic inequality of the moon (an aviator flying from the earth to the sun would require 175 years to make the journey): his probable union in a single mass with the earth in the far-distant past: the probability that in some remote future he will begin to grow colder (there is a turning point in the life of every star): his allotropic variations: his orbital motion: his course through the zodiac: his motion among the stars: his path along the ecliptic: his winged disk: his chariot: his diameter and dimensions: his depth and density, his rotation: his contraction: his daily appearance and disappearance: his image tattooed on my back: his image formed in my mind: the colors of his spectrum as examined with special photographic plates, with a spectroheliograph, with an altazimuth, with a pyrheliometer, with an actionometer, with the bolometer the radiomicrometer, the interferometer: his unhabitability: the festivals held in his honor: the horses sacrificed in his honor: the verses recited in his honor: the dances danced by the Red Indians in his honor: the masks worn by the Aztecs in his honor: the self-torture endured by the Incas in his honor: his importance to the life of the earth, cut off his rays for even a single month and the earth would die: his importance to the life of the soul, cut off his rays for even a single hour and the soul would die: his disturbing influence on the motions of the moon: his attraction for Venus: his turbulence during a Transit of Venus: his contacts with Venus (internal and external) his cosmical significance: his splendor and strength, as symbolised by the seminal energy of the ox: his gold-fingered quietness in late Autumn: his whiteness in the Desert: his cold redness in Winter: his dark and sinister appearance before a Storm: his solid rotundity: his definiteness of form: his politeness in stopping for Joshua: his fasci-nation for Icarus: his importance to the Ancient Mariner: his momentousness to the Prophet: his affiliation with Heliogabalus who married him to the Moon: his mad influence over Aknaton: the reproductions of him by Van Gogh: the reproductions of him on old coins, on the American Twenty-dollar gold piece, (the Eagle and the Sun) on the jackets of jockeys, on soap advertisements, in old wood-cuts, on kindergarten blackboards, on the signs of old taverns: his tremendous influence on religions (among the Vedic Indians, among the Ancient Greeks, among the Ancient Romans, among the Babylonians and Assyrians, among the Ancient Egyptians, among the Hindoos, among the Japanese): the temples erected to his glory (in particular the great sun-temple of Baalbek): his power of con-suming souls: his unconcealed love for sun-dials (true as the dial to the sun): the height he attains at the meridian: his family of asteroids: the occurrence of his name in ornithology, witness the sun bittern (eurypyga helias): among the vertebrates, witness the sun-fish or basking shark: in horticulture, witness the tournesol, the heliotrope, the sunflower (helianthus annus) the marigold and the solsaece (from the word solsequium — sun-following): his light—an uninterrupted continuance of gradation from the burning sunshine of a tropical noon to the pale luminosity that throws no shadow: his faculae and flocculi: his pederastic friendship with the Man in the Moon: the smallness of the target he offers to a meteorite (soul) arrowing toward him from infinity: the different behaviours of his spectral lines which are believed to originate at different levels and the relative Doppler displacements of the same spectral lines as given by his receding and advancing limbs: his importance in the Nebular Hypothesis: his personification in the form of a mirror in Japan: in the form of Ra in Egypt: his halos, rainbows and mirages: his eclipses, in particular the great Egyptian Eclipse of May 17 1882: his nakedness : his red effrontery : his hot-tempered intolerance : his attraction for the earth (equal to the breaking strain of a steel rod three thousand miles in diameter): his temperature (if he were to come as near as the moon, the solid earth would melt like wax): his reflection in the eyes of a girl (perihelion and aphelion): his mountains of flame which thrust upward into infinity : the fantastic shapes of his eruptive prominences (solar-lizards sun-dogs sharp crimson in color) : his brilliant spikes or jets, cyclones and geysers, vertical filaments and columns of liquid flame : the cyclonic motion of his spots : his volcanic restlessness : his contortions : his velocity of three or four hundred miles an hour : his coronoidal discharges : his cyclonic protuberances, whirling fire spouts, fiery flames and furious commotions : his tunnel-shaped vortices : his equatorial acceleration : his telluric storms : his vibrations : his acrobatics among the clouds : his great display of sun-spots : his magnetic storms (during which the compass-needle is almost wild with excitement) : his prominences that have been seen to rise in a few minutes to elevations of two and three hundred thousand miles : his frenzy of turmoil : his periodic explosions : his madness in a lover's heart.

I CLIMB ALONE

I climb alone above the timber line to burn with the setting sun. She is my paramour. Below in the valley the shadows lurk like a pack of wolves. The frozen lake is round like a zero. The smoke of a fire curves upwards into a question mark. The tall firtrees are sentinels guarding the virginity of the mountain. The setting sun disarms them kisses the snow-covered breast of the mountain. And I am jealous and the sun sets. And I leave my flock of stars and wander all night in quest of the lost sun. I am impatient desperate mad. I go swiftly in proud fury. In my haste in the darkness I knock against trees. My body is bruised against boulders. I am frozen by mountain torrents. At last there is a filament of gold. There is the color of the dawn. There is the rising sun burning with gold. She comes towards me as I stand naked on the highest mountain top. The flock of stars have vanished but the Sunstar rises. I feel my eyes filling with fire. I feel the taste of fire in my mouth. I can **hear** fire.

FRAGMENT OF AN ETUDE FOR A SUN-DIAL

let the Sun shine
(and the Sun shone)

on a wooden dial
in the garden of an old castle
(dumb when the Sun is dark)

on a pillar dial
in the Cimetière de l'Abbaye de Longchamp
(blessed be the name of the Sun for all ages)

on the wall of an imaginary house
Rue du Soleil Paris
(the initials of the makers H.C. and C.C. and
date October Seventh 1927 are on the face)
(true as the dial to the Sun)

on a small stone dial
over the door of a farm
(Sole oriente orior
Sole ponente cubo)

on the exterior of a ring dial
worn on the finger of the Princess Jacqueline

("Es-tu donc le Soleil pour vouloir que je me
tourne vers toi?")

on the dial on the south wall
    of a tower
(the Sun is the end of the journey)

and there is a second dial
    on the north wall
(I tarry not for the slow)

on a dial
over an archway in a stableyard
(norma del tempo infallibile io sono)
(I am the infallible measure of the time)

on a dial
in a garden in Malta

on a dial at Versailles

on an old Spanish dial
(the dial has now, 1928, disappeared a
railroad line having been taken through the
garden where it stood)

on the wall of the
Bar de la Tempete at
Breast facing the sea
(c'êst l'heure de boire)

on a small brass dial in
    the British Museum
on a silver dial in the
    Museum at Copenhagen
on a gold dial in the
    soul of a Girl
("mais à mon âme la nécessité de ton âme")

    let the Sun shine
    (and the Sun shone)

on a dial placed upon the
deck of the Aeolus
in the harbor of New London
on a dial placed upon the
deck of the Aphrodisiac
in the harbor of Brest
on a dial placed upon
the deck of the Aurora
in the harbor of my Heart
("et quelques-uns en eurent connaissance")

    let the Sun shine
    (and the Sun shone)

on pyramids of stones
on upright stones in
ancient graveyards
on upright solitary stones
on bones white-scattered on the plain
the white bones of lions in the sun
the white lion is the phallus of the Sun
"I am the Lions I am the Sun"

on the dial of Ahaz who
reigned over Judah

on a rude horologe in Egypt
("as a servant earnestly
desireth the shadow")

on the eight dials of
the Tower of the Winds at Athens

on old Roman coins
unburied from the ground

on the twin sundials on
the ramparts of Carcassone

on the pier at Sunderland
(and where is the sound
    of the pendulum?)

on the sun-dials on the mosques
   of Saint Sophia
   of Muhammed
and of Sulimania

on the immense circular
block of carved porphyry
in the Great Square of
the City of Mexico

on Aztec dials
on Inca dials
(Femme offre ton Soleil en adoration aux Incas)

on Teutonic dials built
into the walls of
old churches

on the dial of the Durer Melancholia
(above the hour-glass and near the bell)

on the white marble slab
which projects from the
facade of Santa Maria Della Salute
on the Grand Canal Venice

on the dial of the Cathedral at Chartres
("the strong wind and the snows")

on a bedstead made of bronze
(and Heliogabalus had one of solid silver)

on a marriage bed
(lectus genialis)
on a death bed
(lectus funebrius)

on a bed
style à la marquise
("ayant peur de mourir lorsque je couche seul")

on a bed
lit d'ange

on a flower bed
on a bed of mother-of-pearl
on a bordel bed
on a bed of iniquity
on a virgin bed
on a bed of rock

To God the Sun Unconquerable
to the peerless Sun, we only

      let the Sun shine
      (and the Sun shone)

      Soli Soli Soli

THE TEN COMMANDMENTS

And the Sun-God spake all these words saying:

I am the Sun thy God which have brought thee out of the land of the Philistine out of the house of bondage.

Thou shalt have no other gods before me.

Thou shalt not be a slave.

Thou shalt never pull down the Flag of Fire.

Remember to be strong and arrogant and lion-hearted. Stamp on the weak.

Remember the pearl of great price.

Honour thy Rimbaud and thy Princess Mad that thy days may be as a comet upon the land which the Sun thy God giveth thee.

Put on the armour of light wield the sword of fury and prepare your bed of delight.

Prehendere, to catch hold of your soul as a talent of pure fire enter into the absolute possession of this fire make a chain to preserve this fire attack to defend this fire.

Be a bird in flight, be an arrow whizzing over their heads.

Thunder with the drum! Blare with the Trumpet of the Future!

Robert Duncan

Born 1919 in Oakland, California. Early along he edited *The Experimental Review* (1940–1941) with Sanders Russell, sharing a concept of the "poem (as) a field of fantastic life . . . an art that involved intensities of the real." But even before *The Venice Poem* of 1948, when he "turned from the concept of a dramatic form to a concept of musical form in poetry," Duncan's voice, as below, was already distinctive, shaped (paradoxically or not) by his "ambition only to emulate, imitate, reconstrue, approximate, duplicate" a line of masters from diverse times, many (particularly among his immediate predecesors) "not everywhere revered." Of these he names "Stein, Lawrence, Pound, H. D., William Carlos Williams, Marianne Moore, Stevens, and Edith Sitwell," and elsewhere adds such moderns as Cocteau, Mallarmé, Yeats, Jack Spicer, Charles Henri Ford, Rilke, Lorca, Kafka, Arp, Max Ernst, St.-John Perse, Prevert, Laura Riding, Apollinaire, Brecht, Mary Butts, Dali, etc.: a list of actual continuities in the system of one intensely aware modern poet, without reference to academic views of the irrelevance, circa 1940, of experimental poetry in the U. S.

Duncan's books before the Black Mountain period were *Heavenly City, Earthly City* (1947), *Poems 1948–9* (1949), & *Medieval Scenes* (1950), some of which turns up with earlier work in *Selected Poems* (City Lights, 1960). A major collection of work written before 1946 is *The Years as Catches* (Oyez, 1966).

I learned that the poem that might be fantastic life, that might be insight into the real, was a rite. The poem was a ritual referring to divine orders.

AN AFRICAN ELEGY

In the groves of Africa from their natural wonder
the wildebeest, zebra, the okapi, the elephant,
have entered the marvelous. No greater marvelous
know I than the mind's
natural jungle. The wives of the Congo
distil there their red and the husbands
hunt lion with spear and paint Death-spore
on their shields, wear his teeth, claws and hair
on ordinary occasions. There the Swahili
open his doors, let loose thru the trees
the tides of Death's sound and distil
from their leaves the terrible red. He
is the consort of dreams I have seen, heard
in the orchestral dark
like the barking of dogs.

Death is the dog-headed man zebra striped
and surrounded by silence who walks like a lion,
who is black. It was his voice crying come back,
that Virginia Woolf heard, turnd
her fine skull, hounded and haunted, stopt,
pointed into the scent where
I see her in willows, in fog, at the river of sound
in the trees. I see her prepare there
to enter Death's mountains
like a white Afghan hound pass into the forest,
closed after, let loose in the leaves
with more grace than a hound and more wonder there
even with flowers wound in her hair, allowing herself
like Ophelia a last
pastoral gesture of love toward the world.
            And I see
all our tortures absolved in the fog,
dispersed in Death's forests, forgotten. I see
all this gentleness like a hound in the water
float upward and outward beyond my dark hand.

I am waiting this winter for the more complete black-out,
for the negro armies in the eucalyptus, for the cities
laid open and the cold in the love-light, for hounds
women and birds to go back to their forests and leave us
our solitude.

*

Negroes, negroes, all those princes,
holding cups of rhinoceros bone, make
magic with my blood. Where beautiful Marijuana
towers taller than the eucalyptus, turns
within the lips of night and falls,
falls downward, where as giant Kings we gatherd
and devourd her burning hands and feet, O Moonbar
there and Clarinet! those talismans
that quickend in their sheltering leaves like thieves,
those Negroes, all those princes
holding to their mouths like Death
the cups of rhino bone,
were there to burn my hands and feet,
divine the limit of the bone and with their magic
tie and twist me like a rope. I know
no other continent of Africa more dark than this
dark continent of my breast.

And when we are deserted there,
when the rustling electric has passt thru the air,
once more we begin in the blind and blood throat
the African catches; and Desdemona, Desdemona
like a demon wails within our bodies, warns
against this towering Moor of self and then
laments her passing from him.

And I cry, Hear!
Hear in the coild and secretive ear
the drums that I hear beat. The Negroes, all those princes
holding cups of bone and horn, are there in halls

of blood that I call forests, in the dark
and shining caverns where
beats heart and pulses brain, in
jungles of my body, there
Othello moves, striped black and white,
the dog-faced fear. Moves I, I, I,
whom I have seen as black as Orpheus,
pursued deliriously his sound and drownd
in hunger's tone, the deepest wilderness.

Then it was I, Death singing,
who bewilderd the forest. I thot him
my lover like a hound of great purity
disturbing the shadow and flesh of the jungle.
This was the beginning of the ending year.

From all of the empty the tortured appear,
and the bird-faced children crawl out of their fathers
and into that never filld pocket,
the no longer asking but silent, seeing nowhere
the final sleep.

The halls of Africa we seek in dreams
as barriers of dream against the deep, and seas
disturbd turn back upon their tides
into the rooms deserted at the roots of love.
There is no end. And how sad then
is even the Congo. How the tired sirens
come up from the water, not to be toucht
but to lie on the rocks of the thunder.
How sad then is even the marvelous!

BERKELEY, 1942

Kenneth Fearing

Born 1902 in Chicago. Died 1961. His use of a long line, easy speech rhythms & the language & symbols of pop culture, to make a new satirizing poetry, remains a presence in the 1950s & 60s, although his own work seems simultaneously to have slipped from view. But it's possible too that an earlier tendency to think of him as a "social poet" has obscured the ominous turns of his mind & his concern with vision & magic, which makes of his last two books (*Afternoon of a Pawnbroker* & *Stranger at Coney Island*) an almost continuous play on the abnormal (= haunted) nature of the "real." The most recent selection of his work was *New & Selected Poems* (1956), which included material from the two books mentioned above, as well as from *Angel Arms* (1929), *Poems* (1935) & *Collected Poems* (1940).

AMERICAN RHAPSODY (2)

First you bite your fingernails. And then you comb your hair again.
    And then you wait. And wait.
(They say, you know, that first you lie. And then you steal, they
    say. And then, they say, you kill.)

Then the doorbell rings. Then Peg drops in. And Bill. And Jane.
    And Doc.
And first you talk, and smoke, and hear the news and have a drink.
    Then you walk down the stairs.
And you dine, then, and go to a show after that, perhaps, and after
    that a night spot, and after that come home again, and climb
    the stairs again, and again go to bed.

But first Peg argues, and Doc replies. First you dance the same dance and you drink the same drink you always drank before.

And the piano builds a roof of notes above the world.

And the trumpet weaves a dome of music through space. And the drum makes a ceiling over space and time and night.

And then the table-wit. And then the check. Then home again to bed.

But first, the stairs.

And do you now, baby, as you climb the stairs, do you still feel as you felt back there?

Do you feel again as you felt this morning? And the night before? And then the night before that?

(They say, you know, that first you hear voices. And then you have visions, they say. Then, they say, you kick and scream and rave.)

Or do you feel: What is one more night in a lifetime of nights?

What is one more death, or friendship, or divorce out of two, or three? Or four? Or five?

One more face among so many, many faces, one more life among so many million lives?

But first, baby, as you climb and count the stairs (and they total the same) did you, sometime or somewhere, have a different idea?

Is this, baby, what you were born to feel, and do, and be?

AGENT NO. 174 RESIGNS

The subject was put to bed at midnight, and I picked him up again at 8 A.M.

I followed, as usual, while he made his morning rounds.

After him, and like him, I stepped into taxis, pressed elevator buttons, fed tokens into subway turnstiles, kept him under close surveillance while he dodged through heavy traffic and pushed through revolving doors.

We lunched very pleasantly, though separately, for $1.50, plus a
   quarter tip. (Unavoidable expense.)
Then we resumed. For twenty minutes on the corner the subject
   watched two shoeshine boys fish for a dime dropped through a
   subway grate. No dice.
And then on. We had a good stare into a window made of invisible
   glass.
Another hour in a newsreel movie—the usual famine, fashions,
   Florida bathing, and butchery. Then out again.
I realized, presently, that the subject was following a blonde dish
   in blue he had seen somewhere around.
(Nothing, ultimately, came of this.)
And shortly after that a small black pooch, obviously lost, attached
   himself to your agent's heels.
Does he fit into this picture anywhere at all?
It doesn't matter. In any case, I resign.

Because the situation, awkward to begin with, swiftly developed
   angles altogether too involved.
Our close-knit atomic world (night would disperse it) woven of
   indifference (the blonde's), of love (the subject's), of suspicion
   (my province), and of forlorn hope (the dog's), this little
   world became a social structure, and then a solar system with
   dictates of its own.

We had our own world's fair in a pinball arcade. The blonde had
   her picture taken in a photomat.
And so (whether by law, or by magnetism) did we.
But still there was nothing, in any of this, essentially new to report.

Except, I began to think of all the things the subject might have
   done, but he did not do.
All the exciting scenes he might have visited but failed to visit, all
   the money I might have watched him make or helped him spend,
   the murders he might have committed, but somehow he re-
   frained.
What if he met a visiting star from the coast? And she had a friend?
Or went to Havana, or the South Sea Isles?

Did my instructions, with expenses, cover the case?
But none of this happened. Therefore, I resign.

I resign, because I do not think this fellow knew what he was doing.
I do not believe the subject knew, at all clearly, what he was look-
ing for, or from what escaping.
Whether from a poor man's destiny (relief and the Bellevue
morgue), or a middle-class fate (always the same job with a
different firm), or from a Kreuger-Musica denouement.
And then, whose life am I really leading, mine or his? His or the
blonde's?

And finally because this was his business, all of it, not mine.
Whatever conscience, boredom, or penal justice he sought to escape,
it was his business, not mine in the least. I want no part of it.
I have no open or concealed passion for those doors we opened
together, those turnstiles we pushed, those levers, handles, knobs.
Nor for the shadow of a bathing beauty on a screen, nor the picture
of a ruined village. Nor any interest in possible defects shown
by invisible glass.
I mean, for instance, I do not (often) feel drawn toward that
particular type of blonde in that particular shade of blue.
And I have no room to keep a dog.

There, this resignation.
Whether signed in a Turkish bath, with a quart of rye, or in a good
hotel, sealed with a bullet, is none of your business. None at all.
There is no law compelling any man on earth to do the same,
second hand.
I am tired of following invisible lives down intangible avenues to
fathomless ends.
Is this clear?
Herewith, therefore, to take effect at once, I resign.

END OF THE SEERS' CONVENTION

We were walking and talking on the roof of the world,
In an age that seemed, at that time, an extremely modern age
Considering a merger, last on the agenda, of the Seven Great Leagues
    that held the Seven True Keys to the Seven Ultimate Spheres
    of all moral, financial, and occult life.

"I foresee a day," said one of the delegates, an astro-analyst from
    Idaho, "when men will fly through the air, and talk across space;
They will sail in ships that float beneath the water;
They will emanate shadows of themselves upon a screen, and the
    shadows will move, and talk, and seem as though real."

"Very interesting, indeed," declared a Gypsy delegate.
"But I should like to ask, as a simple reader of tea-leaves and palms:
How does this combat the widespread and growing evil of the
    police?"

The astrologer shrugged, and an accidental meteor fell from his
    robes and smoldered on the floor.
"In addition," he said, "I foresee a war,
And a victory after that one, and after the victory, a war again."

"Trite," was the comment of a crystal-gazer from Miami Beach.
"Any damn fool, at any damn time, can visualize wars, and more
    wars, and famines and plagues.
The real question is: How to seize power from entrenched and
    organized men of Common Sense?"

"I foresee a day," said the Idaho astrologer, "when human beings
    will live on top of flag-poles,
And dance, at some profit, for weeks and months without any rest,
And some will die very happily of eating watermelons, and nails, and
    cherry pies."

"Why," said a bored numerologist, reaching for his hat, "can't
    these star-gazers keep their feet on the ground?"
"Even if it's true," said a Bombay illusionist, "it is not, like the rope-
    trick, altogether practical."

"And furthermore and finally," shouted the astrologer, with comets
and halfmoons dropping from his pockets, and his agitated
sleeves,
"I prophesy an age of triumph for laziness and sleep, and dreams and
utter peace.
I can see couples walking through the public parks in love, and
those who do not are wanted by the sheriff.
I see men fishing beside quiet streams, and those who do not are
pursued by collectors, and plastered with liens."

"This does not tell us how to fight against skepticism," muttered a
puzzled mesmerist, groping for the door.
"I think," agreed a lady who interpreted the cards, "we are all
inclined to accept too much on faith."

A sprinkling of rain, or dragon's blood,
Or a handful of cinders fell on the small, black umbrellas they raised
against the sky.

Charles Henri Ford

Born circa 1910 in Mississippi. His work, as poet & editor, began with *Blues: A Magazine of New Rhythms* (1929–30), & for nearly two decades he was the principal American advocate of a "surrealist" cultivation of fantasy & dream-time, etc. With all of that, he tried (as the name of that first magazine implies) to work an American, even pop idiom, experimenting as well with found poetry, collage, folk ballad, & photo image. And if he doesn't get it to cohere in his own right, he clearly anticipates a later poetry in which the amalgam works out. Toward that end too, *View* (which he co-edited 1940–47 with Parker Tyler) was one of the mid-40s magazines that maintained the flow between earlier & later avant gardes in America (aided by the World War II presence of André Breton's surrealist government-in-exile). Ford's first book, *The Garden of Disorder*, appeared 1938 with an introduction by William Carlos Williams, & was followed by *The Overturned Lake* (1941) & *Sleep in a Nest of Flames* (1949), selections from both of which are included in *Flag of Ecstasy* (Black Sparrow Press, 1972).

I should like to pick you up, as if you were a woman of water,
hold you against the light and see your veins flow
with fishes; reveal the animal-flowers that rise
nightlike beneath your eyes.

FLAG OF ECSTASY
for Marcel Duchamp

Over the towers of autoerotic honey
Over the dungeons of homicidal drives

Over the pleasures of invading sleep
Over the sorrows of invading a woman

Over the voix céleste
Over vomito negro

Over the unendurable sensation of madness
Over the insatiable sense of sin

Over the spirit of uprisings
Over the bodies of tragediennes

Over tarantism: "melancholy stupor and an uncontrollable desire to
    dance"
Over all

Over ambivalent virginity
Over unfathomable succubi

Over the tormentors of Negresses
Over openhearted sans-culottes

Over a stactometer for the tears of France
Over unmanageable hermaphrodites

Over the rattlesnake sexlessness of art lovers
Over the shithouse enigmas of art-haters

Over the sun's lascivious serum
Over the sewage of the moon

Over the saints of debauchery
Over criminals made of gold

Over the princes of delirium
Over the paupers of peace

Over signs foretelling the end of the world
Over signs foretelling the beginning of a world

Like one of those tender strips of flesh
On either side of the vertebral column

Marcel, wave!

Abraham Lincoln Gillespie

Born Philadelphia in 1895. Died 1950. He moved to Paris in 1922, became a friend of writers like Joyce & Stein, & was for some years a regular contributor to Eugene Jolas' *Transition*. There most of his work took the form of writings on music, theater & dance, but the language throughout was "joycean," as experimental in fact as most of the pieces he wrote about. The "soundpiece" below appeared in *Readies for Bob Brown's Machine* (see page 9), in which Brown had invited other writers to prepare or suggest written work to be viewed via a continuous-flow reading machine. Gillespie's piece singularly grasped the range of the situation & extended it to an investigation of the possibilities of simultaneous performance. In so doing he produced a kind of poem notation that others like Cage & Mac Low would develop at a later time. Unavailable since the days of *Transition*, a selection from his work has been announced for republication by Something Else Press.

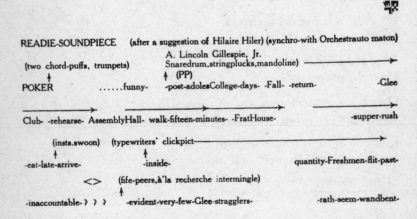

(muHo-chords(bassoons,etc.)devel,30 seconds, a mood-view
↑ chscinto an offkey-thResolution of Accordon&JewsHarp
aiitiii-gone-

-fulfill-YMCA,-nightclass-regs-

ing rhapsody)   (only a Metronome)   (smeasy fiddle-
                       ↑ LENTO   ↑
backstage-   -redescend-dark-redrich-theatre-plush-BoxCorridor- -EldChap-arrive-

-zizzes
                                                                            <
flits-along-side=   -rush-loatHe-despise-Silence-waɪt-acCompany-WONT-talk- -perforce-must

(muted Cornet whinds-in-up then ACCEL.) > out   (low Clarinets)
                                       " Wal-I-see-the-boys-are-back-anybody-outa-this-bunch.

                              (fruity jabbu,lech-timbres-pianissimo <
                              ↑
catch-a-lil-poker-tonite ?"--- he'd-turned-to-me — — — me-curdonvulsed- -his-obstract-

<   SILENCE)   (Accordeon
                                                               ↑
impersonaptriché-glaregloom-pleaVoice   I've-no-memory-of-his-look

grunts sillily)   (one whang-clash of Cymbals,delicato)
                    ↑
       funny........

(dullicate Gongflunets, each ictus) ————————→
                       /
-I-smell-surmise-wopulent-finishalesman'd-Alumnus-   -CampusVisit-   " our-turn-Boys !"

                              (——)
        /   /   /   /
-deerol-Alumnibus-wants-tbe-youngear'd-again I -chap-'bout-midforties-   -willing-lose-

                                                                         (descrip
      /   /   /   /
-careflingly-   -" listen-in-on-rehearsal,-ol'man·   afterwards-Gang-chez-moi

descripMusic,-Orchestra,-'Collegiat Sing Stare Serious' < 'Poko Party'
                                                        ↑ (40-50 secs.)
(Music-sodgo-into-pedalpoint-2-basso-notes-   -superimposed-high-Arabic-wailMelod
                                                      LENTO ————→ dies

-hearable-only-distypewriter-ACCEL.&CRESC.-to-end.

rrettroactinggingg-memries- -seeryussy-Collich-Boys-grimface-barkssiinngg   musikaka-
sonorities-   -friendly-mayaiding-rafters-   dragonfly-airyairplane-stencil-" " Prexy"-
smile-beams-   -postoasty-   -adoliscentious-thoughts-ggoooddaayyss !! !! ....
                   /
       ....chips-   -chipsix-siix-players-mellow-courtly-pal-voices-" correctly"-
hiding-jackal-eeeaggerness-   -PLAY ! -   -two-feelout-post-   -Mr.Jackhill-intrest-deiverted-
I-rememb-regardead-him-once--pass-fleetly----praeterranean-mood-visc-swimface-ghost-
mask-gentility   Mother-guard-your-young-Thru-The-Ages....... !!! ....then >>>> that-
   /   /   /   /   /

third-pot ! ! !   -cards-unlooked-Jackhill's-voice-snapabruptakescharge

(percuss-muted-revolver-shots,each first syllab)   > (aft rubberband
                                                                                                              snapsigh)
OPEN !- -RAISE !- -RAISE !-- -RAISE ! ! ! --   -TREBLE-RAISE ! ! !- -met. . .mutto
(distant speech-voices —————————————————→)
mutto-gurg-suavities-Keep-Tvoice-impent-diabolism- -just-polite-enuf-not-get-nerves

                                                  incl.voices
                                  (Waffle-selling-Cornet < (Absilence)   10 in.rouleau
↑   ↑   (ratchwheel P<F———→)
-SHOWDOWN-. . . . . . . .Jackhill-tops ! !   . . . . .2hrs.-2 more- a half-

                                       Kettle-drums <cymbal>
                                         ↑
'cept-5-6-desultory-pots-Jackhill-W !! !N !S-   WWIINNSSSS ! ! -------w i n s . . . . . .

(Metronome dulls thru the following) —————————→   —————————→
" " allright-fellows-midnight-i-said-i-was-leaving- -rendez-vous-   -you've-studies-
play-tomorrow ? ? ? great ! ! ! -take-this-thirty-bucks. -tomorrow's-drinks-   -let's-have-
a-bang-BangUp ! ! ! !". . . . . ." . . . . . ." . . . . .gap-silence-i-suppose-he-went-out- "-"-geez-
says-Leyden-that-was-funny-almost-phoney-   -why,-his-voice-raising-sounded-GAWN-
satisfahting- -Chirico-horizoning-streetscenes--   -tweren't-human ! ! !. . . . ."   "GWAN-
Bens-ya-silly-mysticketeardrop-twas-only-*his*-turn-(big ! !)-tonite-whheee'll-s-c-a-t-c-him
! ! !. . . . .

PIANO (faintly) streseicts haphazly
↑
nightly-poker-all-week-   -results-same-   -samey-same-   8th-nite-half-hour-before-

Huddle-my-room-(Jim-Armstrong-speaking-)
(Electric Fan joins,nearer)
--" fellers-only-dubs-like-us-get-ridden-like-this-or-would-have-failed-to-saaay-
didn't-any-of-you-notice ? ?-DID-YOU-LOOK-AT-HIS-FACE———CLOSELY ? ! !-I've-been-
talking-things-over-with-a-fratBrother-(P. G.ing-in-Psych)-lissen-from-what-I've-told-
him-he-deduces-that-man-Jackhill-is-a-Visitation-an-Apparition-no-more-corporeal-than-
an-abstraction-or-" Connection"-   -possibly-a-Mesmo-L.C.D.-of o u r -undodesiring-
libidego---no-more-actual-death-than-thought- -in-this-case-thought-incandesced-to-
absolute---NoTime-WILL--a-daemonised-ThwartEcto-of-" DearLife-asked"-Spirilecheality
--creepy-stuff---y'all-look-up-eh ? ?--yeah-as-far-asI-can-see-this-chap-Jackill-i s-
hyprobably-disembodied-Willa-ftDeath-seeking-a LIFErstwhile-unrequited-satisfact ? ?-
Poker-and-get-this-was-in-life-brainKnacktivity-so-dynamicharged-with-PlayLonging-
that-this-tour-de-farce-Luck-at-cards-we' ve-seen-this-week-formerly-meantacted--Will-
to-Accomplish-monoinsanely-carried-over-post-m ortem--became-a-groupswayable-psycometeor-
of-our-Universe--roamoaning-for-Poker (Chordbust <> Astronomic Timbrality Horns &
Percussion)   --gatecrash-punching-" the-hole-in-TimeSpace"-that-Antheil-speaks-about----

----and-we-are-its-pleasure-prey-victims!!! ....probably-an-old-or-recently-
dead-alumnus-of-ours----I'll-make-it-a-point-to-look-oup- ↑ (oboe d'amour&marimba)
the-last-ten-year'-poker-fiends-probably-this-bloke--never-came-near-winning-enu........
IS-SOMEONE-ENTERING-THE-ROOM ? ? ? ....lights-iced-fizzes-highballs-imported-
cigarettes-smoke-hazed-atmoambient---" " cupboard-Link-I'm-off-fellows-
cupboard-slippers-cup "...".......damfool-dank-idèe-fixe----'s been-sounding-in-me

-two-minutes-an-eternity-of-gadfly-dinsistence-wot-liquor!!!----stop-shrieking-
guddemmit-willya ? ? ?---you——————

(MusicBoxes)
↓
well-gang-cupboard-cupboard-guess-Jackhill's-pushed-off-outa-town-leaving-us-cold-
                              cupboard-what's-the-other-term ?   slipboard ?-lippure ?-

losers-I'm-all-for-an-hours-study-then---   one-second-you ?fellows !!! -I-rush-
slippup ?---s--l--i--p---pers!!!!

over-open-my-locked-closet-rummage-shoebag-moneyclink-clashwishpapo-hancluth-emerge-
                                    > (human tune-whistled)

Banknotes-floodChange----STARE -greed-eyes------"↑"look-gang-here s-practically-
the-exact-amount-and-I-should-think-the-identical money-we-all-dropped-in-the-game-
-'cepting-the-thirty-for-tonite's-drinks ------will-each-of-you-figure-out-your-loss-
and-take-it-from-this-little-pyramid----my-losings-were-what-was-left---I-
think-most-of-the-boys-have-never-spoken-about-it-outside-we'd-be-razzed." "

Eugene Jolas

Born 1894 in New Jersey, grew up in Lorraine (France), returned to U. S. A. at 17. Died 1952. From Paris (1927–1938) he edited *Transition*, a comparatively long-lived magazine that acted as a principal link with European modernism (especially Surrealism & related events) & a vehicle for maintaining a consciously numinous & experimental tradition in American poetry between the wars. In all of this his intention was toward a total transformation of language & consciousness in the light of anthropology, psychology, linguistics, folklore, mysticism, etc.; & his enthusiasm for the tantric & gnostic, the primitive & archetypal, if not original with him, would re-emerge as germinal ideas for the poetry & life-ways of the 60s & 70s. Against the force of that continuity, his own poetry seems often spotty, & his language experiments & platforms (verticalism & trilingualism, the revolution of the word, language of night, etc.) naively one-dimensional. Yet when he hits, the "energy" is still a very real presence; & that, I would suggest, is more than can be said for those who chose the safer, middle-ground. The editions of Jolas' poetry, all out of print, are *Cinema* (1926), *Secession in Astropolis* (Black Sun Press, 1929), *I Have Seen Monsters & Angels* (Transition, 1938), *Planets & Angels* (1940), & *Words from the Deluge* (1940); & he was also the editor of *Transition Workshop* (1949).

Revolution of Language
　　(1) An attitude which regards modern language as inadequate for the expression of the changing background of the world, and which posits the necessity of a radical revision of its communicative and symbolical functions.

(2) It regards both the individual creator and the collective folk speech as mediumistic instruments for bringing about the change.

(3) It envisages creative language as a pre-rational process.

MOUNTAIN WORDS

mira ool dara frim
oasta grala drima
os tristomeen.

ala grool in rosa
alsabrume
lorabim
masaloo
blueheart of a

roolata gasta
miralotimbana
allatin

juanilama

RIMBAUD AND THE CHAUFFEUR

Are you afraid of death ? The twilight of the race. We go blindfold through luminous darkness. Black wings. Change the planetary system into a dew drop. It is not a prairie of waves. It is...

An unreal landscape. A cinema. Props appeared and disappeared. I was sitting in a limousine watching the scenes. The changes were vertiginously swift.

A tropical forest. European villages with steeples in the onion-style of the Allemanic baroque churches. A mistagriffe. A roalaroo. Two balas. Motley feathers. Ooras.

The chauffeur a young man. Lyric words. Words that chanted. It was Abyssinian.

— Who are you ?

PROCLAMATION

TIRED OF THE SPECTACLE OF SHORT STORIES, NOVELS, POEMS AND PLAYS STILL UNDER THE HEGEMONY OF THE BANAL WORD, MONOTONOUS SYNTAX, STATIC PSYCHOLOGY, DESCRIPTIVE NATURALISM, AND DESIROUS OF CRYSTALLIZING A VIEWPOINT...

WE HEREBY DECLARE THAT :

1. THE REVOLUTION IN THE ENGLISH LANGUAGE IS AN ACCOMPLISHED FACT.

2. THE IMAGINATION IN SEARCH OF A FABULOUS WORLD IS AUTONOMOUS AND UNCONFINED.
(Prudence is a rich, ugly old maid courted by Incapacity... Blake)

3. PURE POETRY IS A LYRICAL ABSOLUTE THAT SEEKS AN A PRIORI REALITY WITHIN OURSELVES ALONE.
(Bring out number, weight and measure in a year of dearth... Blake)

4. NARRATIVE IS NOT MERE ANECDOTE, BUT THE PROJECTION OF A METAMORPHOSIS OF REALITY.
(Enough ! Or Too Much !... Blake)

5. THE EXPRESSION OF THESE CONCEPTS CAN BE ACHIEVED ONLY THROUGH THE RHYTHMIC " HALLUCINATION OF THE WORD ". (Rimbaud).

6. THE LITERARY CREATOR HAS THE RIGHT TO DISINTEGRATE THE PRIMAL MATTER OF WORDS IMPOSED ON HIM BY TEXT-BOOKS AND DICTIONARIES.
(The road of excess leads to the palace of Wisdom... Blake)

7. HE HAS THE RIGHT TO USE WORDS OF HIS OWN FASHIONING AND TO DISREGARD EXISTING GRAMMATICAL AND SYNTACTICAL LAWS.
(The tigers of wrath are wiser than the horses of instruction... Blake)

8. THE " LITANY OF WORDS " IS ADMITTED AS AN INDEPENDENT UNIT.

9. WE ARE NOT CONCERNED WITH THE PROPAGATION OF SOCIOLOGICAL IDEAS, EXCEPT TO EMANCIPATE THE CREATIVE ELEMENTS FROM THE PRESENT IDEOLOGY

10. TIME IS A TYRANNY TO BE ABOLISHED.

11. THE WRITER EXPRESSES. HE DOES NOT COMMUNICATE

12. THE PLAIN READER BE DAMNED.
(Damn braces ! Bless relaxes !... Blake)

— *Signed* : KAY BOYLE, WHIT BURNETT, HART CRANE, CARESSE CROSBY, HARRY CROSBY, MARTHA FOLEY, STUART GILBERT, A. L. GILLESPIE, LEIGH HOFFMAN, EUGENE JOLAS, ELLIOT PAUL, DOUGLAS RIGBY, THEO RUTRA, ROBERT SAGE, HAROLD J. SALEMSON, LAURENCE VAIL.

— Arthur Rimbaud.

Were you sceptical about him ? He seemed so different from the *Illuminations*. The nightworld of his eyes. Yet the War...

Rimbaud word-chanted : *Le Bateau Ivre*. He was wearing a battered khaki uniform of the American soldier. He drunken-sang : *Je suis un négrier du roi Négus*...

He no longer wore his uniform. A monk's cassock much too large for him. He turned around and said :

— *Le cinéma est mort.*

SLEEP IN UR
(DREAM-SCENARIO)

First Part

A long white road.
Poster in blue, white and black :
   WHEN YOU GO TO NEW YORK
   STAY AT THE BUCKINGHAM
A masked man.
Automobile crashing along at mad speed. Roar of motors.
The sun blazes down.
An old farm-house long ago abandoned.
Alfalfa fields.
The automobile races through village.
Main Street.
Radio jazz-splashing on pavement.
Electric train clangs through valley.

Second Part

Columbus Circle.
X arrives in automobile with an enormous perch, in form of a cross, but obviously in its original form a totem-pole.
Sultry July dusk.
Crowd milling around Maine Monument.
Automobile motors whir.
X carries his totem-cross into music store.

A sound of jazz from jug-band.
Feet of passers-by become epileptic
X runs across square crying :

>Larvae wool moult
>Aluminium hulls
>Sing throats of steel
>Sing tongues of nickel !

A sound like electric waves cuts into the nerves of the passers-by.

Blood sputters on the asphalt.
A voice chants a Congo song.
Screen changes suddenly into luminous colors of every description. The new moon tumbles down. A planet burns rose against a poster for United States Rubber.

X carries his totem-cross and hums a folk-song.
X places totem-cross against street-lamp.
Crowd rushes by with a kind of hallucinated step, very staccato, monotonous, almost disciplined.

X suddenly notices a Mayan corpse, withered and waxen, hanging on totem-cross.

What is it ?

Third Part

July night on Rialto.
Times building trembles as if under the shock of earth-quake.
Crowd mangles Broadway singing :

>Our little moon is dead !
>Our little star's gone out !
>O clingaling o clang !
>O putrid phantom rout !

X walks out of subway station with totem-cross over his shoulders.

A girl begins to dance at the curb.
The crowd sways rhythmically. There is a feeling of erotic mass-insanity in the air.

A masked man.
X throws perch into waiting automobile.
Electric lights glare against a huge zodiac sketched upon a poster.

They shine full blast into the face of the corpse on the totem-cross.

A shriek.

X runs to the car, where several women stand in a trance of horror.

The eyes of the withered Mayan divinity have opened.

Close-up of eyes : enormous, circular, metallically blue.

They roll in a feverish intensity.

Bells ring.

Auto claxon roars crescendo.

The houses lean over the pavement like drunken men.

Fourth Part

Night.

Telegram arrives :

> X   Hotel Buckingham, New York.

Diabolical events stir sleep stop Tom-Tom astrologer Stop Nightingales rock drunken last vertigo Stop Locusts devastate ruins legends Stop Alone Desperate Z.

The Mayan divinity appears. It is now huge of stature and clad in evening clothes.

X — his face blanched by fear. Rats scurry around his feet.

X talks excitedly to Y, the resurrected corpse.

" Where to ? "

" Saturn... "

" How ? "

" On swinging carpet of love. "

X thinks : "...Taxi... Help... Singing away... Carnival... War Help... "

Jazz orchestra.

Telephone : "Hello... District Attorney's Office...; Hello. Police Headquarters. Revolution... Fire Department... Hello... Fire... Red Rooster... Hello... City Hall... Anarchy... Insanity... Hello... Hello... " X reads Daily Tarot :

TAXI DANCER IN POISON CASE

O'DONNELL GETS	OCEAN OF LOVE
UP TO 50 YEARS	ROUGH, SINGER
IN RAPE CHARGE	LANDS IN RENO

VILLAGE COWED
BY GANG PATROL
IN BANK LOOTING
JOHNNY WALKER WALKS THE PLANK
DON'T MISS THESE FEATURES IN TODAY'S SUNDAY
TAROT.
CUT THE HAIR OR LET IT GROW
OTHER NEWS IN TABLOID

X walks out followed by Y who waves his arms and whistles between his teeth.

Fifth Part

Midnight, Brooklyn Bridge.

X tells Y : " ...Leave me alone... Go down the tracks... Alone... Aged solitude... ".

Y snickers. His laughter develops into a sneer. It grows into an insane cackling that resounds above the noise of the elevated train just passing.

X looks at lower Manhattan. The city gleams in clustered cliffs of jewels.

X : Mendacity of fairy-tales...

Y : Xipe Totec...

X : Colibris haunt the strangled bodies...

Y : Mother night...

X : raging and foaming at the mouth like epileptic in convulsions.

Y sneers.

X attacks Y, pins his arms behind his back, cries: Acheronta movebo.

An old hag treasurepicks in garbage can.

Picture of Roman funeral lamp with orphic illustrations of baby in golden vessel before a caterpillar and a butterfly.

Y turns into corpse once more.

His face is tranquil, almost angelic ; the eyes look into space as if at some ecstatic vision.

A child sleeping in cradle.

Sixth Part

A masked man, a crippled dwarf, a penguin.

An over-voice cries : The sorcerer of alchemy is dead...

And always there will be parallactic instruments...

X, his shoulders hunched, walks into a milk-white fog, saying :

                Woman is sleep
                Healing like rain
                Primal νοῦς
                And mantic pain

Two steel eyes gyrate prestissimo.

The over-voice again, a shrill, electric sound, growing in intensity until the fog is torn by an asteroid shaft of light.

From EXPRESS

Mysterious fingers shake the atlas over which I have walked in many midnights, when the old house listened to the snarl of the wind.

I ride on the clinking rails, and my eyes wait for elegies bright as a spring morning in New York.

Metallic fairy tales fill my space, the frontiers crackle into ashes, the voices which burst through darkness are mute.

New in my hands is hope, and love pulsing around the zodiac drinks the tears of the humble women in the city streets.

I am on my way to the asphalt, where acrobats move before the verb, and I leave behind the trance of afternoons strange with explosions of silence.

O tantum ergo of winged dusk!

The forests still dream into bells, into herb, into humming, into sun and listen to magical fugues.

Villages surge up, gabled and grey, with belfries rearing evangels into the bluest skies.

But the wheels beat time to our desires and to the kyrie eleison of concrete.

Subway trains smashing into trembling stations echo in my mind with the chant of a huge city by the sea.

The prison moves staccato into the desert of stone.

And soon we will see glint over roofs, over avenues, over motors, over cathedrals, over nights anarchic with dreams.

And we will go through sleep towards phantom halls to a love past understanding.

We slink through a sleeping town and the walls of the old houses suddenly rise into pallor.... I've gotta love that girl till I die.

Do not lean over the parapet, my hermetic friends : The antelope drifts across the fields seeking the cavern of vanished secrets.

The villages are mute with soliloquies. So let us sail, the forests whip around us, the eyes of the hare are broken.

Hold high your head, my lady, a baboon wings towards you, indolent swoon of the knees. Are we alone again ?

The slope withers with heather. The acre steams. What clusters about the vagabond who gazes at the convulsions of the loco-motive ?

Light comes ringing from invisible beatitudes.

I remember the milltown in snow-storms and a girl beside me, weeping.....

The road is a disk, the sheep turn on the effigies, I cry over the whir of agonizing monotones. Shall we take the clockwork apart again ?

Keep silence, diadem ! The letter was a lie. Our enemies crouch in the half-light of the distant street-lamp.

The old man standing in the doorway of his stable nods into autumn. The church is a dark signal.

The telegraph poles sing like a sirocco, shutters enclose dreams, the fetish shrieks in the shadows.

Birds lie crushed in the road through which the last pilgrim passed so long ago, and where the gipsy wagon tarries in the gloom.

I have hated too much in the darkness of my solitude.

III

The bells have ceased their tinkle and the cargo stirs in the casks and barrels, where the miles illuminate our vision.

How long will you be here; moon-glistering dynamo ?

The Corn-Mother weeps in the nearby fields. The wings of my sadness flew over chimney-pots and huts, and the oil-lamp swaled.

Winds come down the road-bed sniffing the carcass of the dog. I am haggard from mould of silences.

The tracks are sharp as sickles and the cassocked skeletons wander down the field-path, and the girls hold tryst with the dusk.

An old man wanders up and down the platform, it is so lonely here, the young girl gets on board to tempt the lights of the boulevards.

The station-master winks at his wife, and hunters carrying mutilated deer stare down the tracks.

We race through a luminous foam, and the clock ticks off the minutes with a whimper.

The kermesse ends in a din, all the men and women stop their smiles, the cafés grow dark.

Why do I think of Coney Island hot with an afternoon in July and the wet skins of the East-Side women dripping in the sand ?

Paradise stops its music. Black animals crawl through the trees. The flight of blossoms cries.

Listens to the incantations on the road ! The honeycombs have disintegrated, and the offerings are in vain.

The stories go on in the child's sleep endless like a rosary mumbling.

We stand before a cannonade and night is Vitzliputzli waiting for sacrifice.

Again that sound of waters rushing through the locks.

Again the interplanetary speed.

IV

There is no more talk. All the mouths are pinched with waiting. These brains are filled with brothels, electric signs, rack of streets.

Nearer we come to the conflagrations. Lightning will strike in the sky of the sorrows.

Where are you going, strangers and friends, your eyes are fatigued and your bags lie rotting in the sinister cabal.

You have never known the liberty I cried for, when the night came roaring out of nowhere, and the landscape fled from the lanterns.

The wheels click-click through the plains, the tracks are mutilated with destinies, the sod smokes with insects.

A woman yawns, her teeth are filled with maggots. The stalks on the stubblefields nod with fear. We are also afraid.

In a Paris café I met a green-eyed woman who smiled into the absynthe shimmer of her memories. A song lay dead on her lips.

We are prisoners straining away from dementia, and our hearts beat for the adventures of the straits of Zoolibar.

Smile, damn you, smile, the plain is in panic.

For life is still a grave, a pine-forest, a crow, a gipsy, a requiem, while we wing towards the east.

We look once more at the prophecy of a crucifixion.

And a city waits for us with gifts more luminous than tropical forests.

v

I am a dream-man in a chaos.

Rain shakes the windows, as I watch the tortured beings waste into decay....

Chase yourself, little specter of the night !

The air quakes with the echoes of the bombs which the stars shot down.

Our loneliness is more terrible than that of a prison. If I should shout, no one would hear my voice, and my words would come back scorched into shame.

The movement of the cars piling up into distorted pyramids crashes against the evanescent twilight.

How strange it was, landing in Brooklyn one winter dusk, as the bridges swung their cables over the sea-hungry river !

Faces sink against me like gulls, grey faces and cancerous cheeks, and lovely roses of girls.

Come into me, rigid dream, and stay with me ! Feet clack into the mythos of my wonderings. And always the monotone of the wheels.

I am no longer a man of flesh and bone. I go bursting into the moving space fogging itself around me.

I go singing into the smoke and hurl myself into visionary expectancies. The sighs of the palm-trees are far away.

Lonely sky falls over my eyes, and the forehead of the voyager reeks against my hands.

Immense will be the witches' sabbath bringing the demented guitars and the seven wonders of the world.

Walter Lowenfels

Born 1897 in New York City. He lived in Paris during the late 1920s, where he joined with writers like Henry Miller, Anais Nin & Michael Fraenkel in a self-described "death school." With that consciousness as central focus, he did important work in long forms, toward construction of a trilogy called *Some Deaths*, which appeared in installments (*Apollinaire*, *Elegy for D. H. Lawrence*, & *The Suicide*) between 1930 & 1932. In the mid–30s Lowenfels left poetry for radical politics, was for years the Pennsylvania editor of *The Daily Worker*, & was prosecuted & convicted (though conviction later overturned) under the Smith Act of the 1950s. He has since returned to poetry, along with the editorship of a number of politically oriented anthologies & several books of his own shorter poems, letters, essays, etc. Other works from the Paris period & before include *Epistles & Episodes* (1925), *Finale of Seem* (1929), & a play, *U. S. A. with Music* (1930). His death-trilogy has never been republished as a whole, although the Lawrence poem appeared in *We Are All Poets, Really* (1968), & one- or two-page versions of that & *Apollinaire* appeared in the Jargon Press "selected poems," also called *Some Deaths*, in 1964.

Death is the moral force of the world. Our danger isn't that we are going suicidal, but that we are not. We haven't created anything to kill . . . .
(W. L., 1929)

> *By continual suicide*
> *I escaped being similar to myself*
> *which is*

I lived
too slowly
the something else that was always me.

APOLLINAIRE AN ELEGY

It is enough that the night
is full of rain and chimes and angels
like a Spanish cathedral
        with the street
an escala d'oro
the stars descend.

Forgive the word O Builder
        the poem was between the rain and
                the chimes
    not in the word but in the angels.

Yours O Apollinaire was an act.
Your name has the sound of a statue
or a temple the eyes have not seen.

The columns of Baalbek crumble
        architecture remains
like a dream of the world.

Building is a vista or a vision
a spirit that inhabits stone or air
the persistent soul of objects
making any everything
a womb of possibilities.

And green is green !
    And cream is cabbages
                and red are carrots.
How lovelier than Miss Universe
to live on vegetables and colour that make
each truck lumbering through the rain

a chariot of the Lord.
Lamp posts are golden with the eyes of God
and Apollo drives the horses of the sun
down the street to collect loud garbage

    a thousand departures
for the thousand poems in the mind
and
                        at Burgos
                                the hill

where the Cid persists in grass-eaten stone
    goats ranging the ruined battlements
the mangy couple
making a palace of the broken moat

                        O Spring
still Spring
          forever Spring

  white violets growing there

still blooming wild

            creating still
the mind's persisting Spring.

    And why the oppression of weeping without weeping
    at the emigrants qui
    emplissent de leur odeur le hall de la Gare St-Lazare ?
    There is also a theology of gas mains.

    Good-bye
           far away
               good-bye.
    There shall be songs of the Argentine

        but in the other sense
    you lie still.

We can give you nothing
but what we take
                    there's
the cold comfort of objective immortality.
No more the burial with flints.
The witch doctors have gone
                              with them
the obscure hopes of earlier Christs.
No more the white bird rises invisibly
to carry the soul from sight.
                              For us
the purity of extinction.
Not even Mr. Ford shall lie
with a thousand piston rings
to feed his soul in heaven.

Statistics rule a million millions
the oppression of whose certain numbers
leaves their dying epic as an almanac
and no sadder than the census of East St. Louis.
Tragedy is one
        and one is a poet.

Mort à Guillaume ! Mort à Guillaume !
In the street
                below
the mob were shouting
for another William.

It was Armistice Day. The war was over.
In the room a known soldier died.
One voice said *Il l'a coupé*.
From the street
                the crowds
shouting *Mort à Guillaume*.

This grave stands for no millions.
Here no strangers lay wreaths.
Here no light burns eternally but our own.

His Arc de Triomphe is a structure of the world
not in the word but in the angels
and every taxi horn of Paris
keeps his flame eternally rekindled
not in the sound but in the angels.

His is a continual creation
leading yesterday into tomorrow
making every poem that is a poem
a monument wherein his flame
lights outward the world's plasticity
not toward the word but toward the angels.

It is possibilities
whose unfulfilled passing
obey the laws of tragedy.
                          For mourning
dying is not enough.
There is a logic of death.

We'll visit the graves of all who died too young
to mourn for what we might have known.

This shall be one-soul's day
building its own sorrow
into the gaping body of the earth.

Other deaths
                for other theologies.

This day we mourn this man
because the world
                     and our world
is less one possibility
still unlisted
in the tables of insured certainty.

We sold liberty bonds in Little Rock, Ark.
We were betrayed on the Russian Front.

WALTER LOWENFELS · 163

Leave us brother
we lived only for this.
We are the dead and the alive
We enjoyed the smell of being one of many.
We lived for that
and thus for this.
We overcame our destiny and remained
the human race.
We are the millions of heros
                    we lie here as heros do.
We do not know
the tragedy of peace.
Only we know
our dying was a formality
        not an event.

Leave us brother
        leave us our war
we *lived* in that
and thus
for this.

        Rot his bones
                    scatter his flesh
            he wants nothing from death
        but death.
        It will not fail him that.

        O astronomer move out our stars
        light us more light years
                            say
        what we see from Mt. Wilson
        is Mt. Wilson and heaven and us
                more heaven on earth than there's in heaven
        but from my nose
        take away this dead fish
        of the immortality of the soul.
        And O Cholera blight this cult
        who make death a fetich

worn in the lapel
like a rotten rose
    who see adventure in extinction
sensation in futility
exitement in worms
        who seek death to live.

This is his purgatory
                    and ours
        a later Christ and the Kingdom
                        within
burning its own ashes by its own flame :
Phoenix
            alive :
dead
        dead.

O Few
        O Poets
                    mourn for Apollinaire.
He has sunk and will not rise
                            and still
        through the rainy nights of Paris
moves his unuttered poem
                        and lives
still lives in the mind's persisting Spring.

    He leaves dead death
to be a later revelation of the world
        he mounts into the rain
                            into the night
not like Lycidas into the darkened heavens
but in the moving glitters of the street
he shines a later and lost star.

Weep for the untraced interstellar spaces of a wet pavement.
Weep weep astronomers for a lost poem a lost world.
Weep for you will dot infinity with nebulae
and leave forever unrecorded
the infinity that surrounds the passing footfall

WALTER LOWENFELS · 165

that might have been a diapason of angels
in the singing kingdom of Apollinaire.

Each man to his own dead
and grief that returns with the revolving year
but this death is more than death
    the earth is truly wet with rainy eyes
the world is mourning the world's own death
dying in its own creation in Apollinaire.

Weep weep O world. . . . .
                      I am silent in this sorrow.
This is a service of the rain
           and the muffled drum of a footfall
and the chimes
          and the angels.

   The city shrivels into darkness
facing a black stone desert toward the day.
A dearth of angels
                warps the hours
that curl back into clocks
while Time waits in a coma for the sun.
A dearth of angels
              strips the city to gutters
   and
walls the night
    blackness in blackness
                 stone in stone
   and
leaves a heart beat and a heart beat
strangers to the world company for me.
A dearth of angels
           drifts down like a parachute
on to the brain
         and leaves
it shrouded in its bleakness
and the world in its
    the world to the world and me to me.
A dearth of angels

                    and
          the dirge disintegrates to one and one and
                                        one and one
                    less
          the illuminating analysis of a conjunction . . .

Not the word breaks
but the thought
          not the tongue decomposes
but the brain
          not that thinking is too much
but the mind goes wormy . . . . .

                    O Anathema
          on those shrivelers of the earth
                    leaving it beyond seed
          a dried bean on a withered stalk
          firelessly baked into tasteless hard-tack.

          Better the revulsion of worm-white meat
                    the activity of disgust
          than your drab slab
          of inexistence
                    seeing fresh pulp
          as old tar
                    losing the ecstasy of disaster
          for a dry doom.

          How meagre for company
                    whose despair is a wisp of hollow straw
          trickling a thin dribble of death
                    starvation diet for a flea.
          Better be a care-free louse
          than a bloodless shell
                                        displaying
          the appurtenances of a crab
                    without claws
                    without meat
                    without motion
          (gone even is the vestige of a sideway scuttle).

How puny your sorrows
        an itching pimple
        irritation of a scab
        sadness of a skin disease
escaping the tragedy of resistance
in an ointment of quick despair
        (sometime
warbling bad sweetness
like an automatic violin
        in a glass case
responding to the nip of any nickel).

Here is something deserted on a beach
lost between a picnic and an ocean
bleached from the slight contact
of too much too little
losing even the last faint odour
        in a last aridity.

O false shell
                false suffering
crying the name for the deed
how tenacious is your brittleness
glazed to a fake eternity
        a dump of hair pins
                corset covers   old cans
(past this wasted frontier
deep is the green country
full of bark and pines).

Better be fungus
                and dot
the dark hollow places
the spaces between roots
and give at least a plop
as you squash out
        when stepped on.

I have seen the trains stand still moving
while I move out standing still.
Toward thee O death are all my journeys
                        but the mind bends toward an eye
                                    that lives in a lamp post
and lights this night
with an x to mark the spot
of its constantly moving horizon.

> . . . . . in North Dakota
>   the night-rising ducks
>   over the mounds
>   blocking the moon
>   burning out
>   still
>   blooming wild
>   in the mind's persisting Spring.

   O Brain !
in thinking itself there's an excellence of act
that makes a sacrement of processes.

Yours Apollinaire was an act.
Yours is moving world my mind has rested in.
I do not weep at the Gare St-Lazare
but I am moved when I move with you
through the millions in this building
    into building
away from the stale odour of a million nouns
(even now they sleep the sleep of the righteous
while the sparrows are beginning
to look for crumbs and chant Laus Deo
like a choir of early acolytes
chirping in a new day).

      To you
for saving a night
for having been
                    for being

throughout the drizzling dark
a priest and a prophet
saying while you say the Seine is there
pointing out pointing out the Eiffel Tower there
that poetry is this and that
          living
             there.

You who were Provence to those who went before
came into being again
to be Apollinaire to us
        showing to those who saw
                 those who see
a way to build

    making your going out
a coming in

    saying
that death that is the act
is a passing at the point of a possible beginning
making anywhere a beginning
any point a possibility

saying
the world is constantly building
dying into beginning
    saying
the world is enough
and that is enough.

Jackson Mac Low

Born 1922 in Chicago, moved to New York City circa 1943. A musician from his early years, he would later introduce systematic chance operations, simultaneity, asymmetric structure, & serial techniques into poetry, with a strong sense of method as process that would make him the most innovative & most formal poet of the 1960s. But his work also sums up & extends the experiments of many earlier *avant garde* poets—of some of whom he was in fact a younger contemporary—& itself shows a movement from chance as "automatic writing" (below) to chance as "random composition," where "random," as in statistics, "applies to special techniques for eliminating bias in sampling." (G. Brecht) And Mac Low, as part of his contribution to the elimination of "bias" (of the individual imposing his will on the world), early places his own work in a Buddhist & "anarchist" succession, in which the poet, "preeminently the maker of the plot, the framework—not necessarily of everything that takes place within that framework . . . creates a *situation* wherein he invites other persons & the world in general to be co-creators with him! He does not wish to be a dictator but a loyal co-initiator within the free society of equals which he hopes his work will help to bring about."

Still underpublished (though extensively performed & self-performed), Mac Low's major works in print include 22 *Light Poems* (1968, & *Stanzas for Iris Lezak* (1972), along with *An Anthology*, a compendium of late 50s / early 60s *avant garde* performance pieces, which he edited with La Monte Young in 1963. "H U N G E R-ST r i kE," printed below, was written at age 16 & first published thirty years after the event in John Logan's *Choice* (1968). Other early works are yet to appear.

m/mp	*And now by chance— /r/f/ O blessed chance continue to happen to me!* ½
s/p	*For I wd never plan so well— /r/mp/ I wd have died of my planning—* ½
mr/mf	*A new happiness has come which I never cd have imagined—* 2½
m/mp	*A new happiness which may not last at all* ½
r/mf	*For all happiness that happens to us passes as all happenings do—* ½
vs/mp	*But while it is here—now—* 2
m/p	*I thank you* ½
m/mf	*I thank you* ½
m/f	*I thank you* 5

(1960)

H U N G E R ST r i kE wh A t doe S   lifemean

h

Water and water and water and water
Whater you thinking about
Or are you doing
what areyou doing
Fire in grates are greates
Ingrates in grate
great ingrates in great grate
great grate greasy great grate
grating
g r a v e r l o w
        GRATE
God and god and god and god
G r o d an d grod in grate
in great ingrate in grate in great grate
Growl great grate
Grin g r o w l i n ggreat grate
Great grown ing grateS
Grod and grod and grod and grod

        A N D   G R O D

        G L O W
        ———————

GLORY GLOW

g l o r y and g lor y and g lory andglory

G R Ơ U C H
-- -- -- -- --

Grow grouc h
G r o w and grow and grow andgrow

A n d   Grow   (grunt)
Great gracious grunt

G O   and go a n D
go   go g o gogo go
go   go go go
              G O   D
              _____

Go god go god go
   g o d   g o g o D

              O   G O D
              _____

              _____

g ain   g a m e s gain
            g a m es
g a i n   g a y   gam e S
g-ame   gain games

G o L l Y god agog agog
gog gog goggog g o g gog gog gog

              G R O G
              _____

G R U C H   g r u c h gruch
   g r a g   gr ag   grag

              g l u g
              _____

And the bathtub went down the drain
Ukraine

Cranium Ukrainium
        (Uranium)
Xi You cranium crane
Crane yum you crane
You crane Ukraine
Krake and krake and krake and krake and cake (krake)
G a k e^{gage}cake   gag gag gaggag gaggaggaggag gag
                g o n g
gog gog   gawg   gawg   gawg
                goug goug

                G O D   (cod)
                _____

Gay cake gotta gay cake go gotta gay cake
gaga gotta gay cake
gong gong gonk

                God in his mercy is good
                God in his mercy is good
                God in his mercy is good
                God in his mercy is good
                God in his mercy is good
                God in his mercy is good
                God in his mercy is good
                God in his mercy is good
                God in his mercy is good
                God in his mercy is good
                God in his mercy is good
                God in his mercy is good
                God in his mercy is good
                God in his mercy is good
                God in his mercy is good
                God in his mercy is good
                God in his mercy is good
                God in his mercy is good
                God in his mercy is good
                God in his mercy is good
                God in his mercy is good
                God in his mercy is good
                God in his mercy is good
                God in his mercy is good
                God in his mercy is good
                God in his mercy is good
                God in his mercy is good
                God in his mercy is good
                God in his mercy is goog
                Gog in his mersy iz goog

```
          Gog im fis merky ib goog
          Gog ig gis mergy ig goog
          Gog ig gig gergy ig goog
          Gog ig gig giggy ig goog
          Gog gg ggg ggggy gg goog
          Gog gg ggg ggggg gg gggg
          ggg gg ggg ggggg gg gggg
          gggggggggggggggggggggggg
```

```
ggggggggggggggggggggggggggggggggggggggggggggggggggggggggggggggggggggggggggggggggggggg
```

```
ston ston tont tont ston stant stont stint stit
        Hi stonet stont stit
stit stlit stlod stlott stlit stlodstlott
  stloff stlow slow slow slowly
slow       slow       slowbly
       s l a b l y       s l o w ly
s l o w b l y
    slob  blob
blob  blob  blob
blob  blob blob blos blop
blob blob blobg blog
b r a g     b r i m     b r a g
b r a g     brimming    brrraag
        b l o o g l y       blagly
```

```
    blagly bloogly
bland   blagly bloogly
       bloogly  -long
```

```
                    Blong
                    Blong
                    Blong
```

```
        g
```

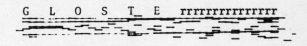

```
G l a b b e r   glabber glabber
glad to be of service
so glad to be of service
sinfully glad to be of serrice
```

                    for his hit surface
                         (surflakes)

good guy can't carry cash
          crash
good guy can't carry cash
cood cguy cgan't gary gpash

g la ss   g la ss   g la ss   g la ss   g la ss
                                                                  (gloss)

                         g   r   o   u   c   h

Can't go
Can't go carry nothing
scant   ko   scary   sluthing
                         s   l   o   p

slinguliar slop
        slaresly   slasely

        slap   slap   slap
                      slooker

                         ₤

                    S   L   A   P
                         SLANK

                    ─────────────────────

                    ─────────────────────

plap plaster plap psplap

                              prask

                                   pony

Charles Olson

Born 1910 in Worcester, Mass. Died 1970. His first important poetry publication, *Y & X* (1948), was the last book from Harry & Caresse Crosby's Black Sun Press. The later move to Black Mountain College (1951–56) & appearances in Cid Corman's *Origin* & Robert Creeley's *Black Mountain Review* were the occasion, David Antin writes, for "the reappraisal of Pound and Williams, the return of Rexroth, Zukofsky, and the later return of Oppen, Rakosi, Reznikoff and Bunting." And, he adds, "it was quite appropriate for Williams to reprint Olson's essay on 'Projective Verse' in his own autobiography, because it was the first extended discussion of the organizational principles of this wing of modernist poetry." What Olson made clear, as others for their own concerns, was that this was no *ex nihilo* brainstorm but a comment on "the already projective nature of verse," a development inherited in his view from "Cummings, Pound, Williams," etc., with 1930s "objectivism" as the nearest point of connection. Renaming that insight "objectism," he described it as "the getting rid of the lyrical interference of the individual as ego, of the 'subject' and his soul, that peculiar presumption by which western man has interposed himself between what he is as a creature of nature (with certain instructions to carry out) and those other creations of nature which we may, with no derogation, call objects." And there too (in the getting rid of ego, while "staying inside," to know oneself as object) was not only the Williams-Pound connection but, as others would grasp it, links to a process, of emptying & filling, that has been the "organizing principle," the spiritual force of "modernism," in its most diverse & significant projections.

"The K," below, was "written in ca. early 1945" & first appeared in *Y & X*. It can be found in *Archaeologist of Morning*

(1971), "which contains every poem Charles Olson authorized for publication in his lifetime, apart from the *Maximus* sequence."

It comes to this: the use of a man, by himself and thus by others, lies in how he conceives his relation to nature, that force to which he owes his somewhat small existence. . . . If he stays inside himself, if he is contained within his nature as he is participant in the larger force, he will be able to listen, and his hearing through himself will give him secrets objects share.

THE K

Take, then, my answer:
there is a tide in a man
moves him to his moon and,
though it drop him back
he works through ebb to mount
the run again and swell
to be tumescent I

The affairs of men remain a chief concern

We have come full circle.
I shall not see the year 2000
unless I stem straight from my father's mother,
break the fatal male small span.
If that is what the tarot pack proposed
I shall hang out some second story window
and sing, as she, one unheard liturgy

Assume I shall not.
Is it of such concern when what shall be
already is within the moonward sea?

Full circle: an end to romans, hippocrats and christians.
There! is a tide in the affairs of men to discern

Shallows and miseries shadows from the cross,
ecco men and dull copernican sun.
Our attention is simpler
The salts and minerals of the earth return
The night has a love for throwing its shadows around a man
a bridge, a horse, the gun, a grave.

1945

George Oppen

Born 1908 in New Rochelle, N. Y. Grew up in San Francisco. With his wife, Mary Colby, he went to France circa 1929 & there founded To Publishers (later the Objectivist Press) in co-editorship with Louis Zukofsky. Published Zukofsky's "*Objectivists*" *Anthology*, Pound's *ABC of Reading*, Williams' *Collected Poems 1921–1931*, along with work by himself & Charles Reznikoff, among the main "objectivist" poets. Oppen's own work from that time comprises a small volume, *Discrete Series* (1934), after which he became a Communist labor organizer & took, he says elsewhere, 25 years to write his next poem. But the work shows, for all of that, a remarkable continuity of attentions—a concern with structure ("the objectification of the poem, the making an object of the poem") & with the process that informs that structure (the poem as "a test of truth" or "test of images . . . of whether one's thought is valid, whether one can establish a series of images, of experiences . . . whether or not one will consider the concept of humanity to be valid, something that is, or else have to regard it as simply being a word"). From all of which there finally emerges a poetry in which the "virtue of the mind is that emotion which causes to see."

The selection below reproduces the complete *Discrete Series*, though the spacing between sections has been greatly reduced; therefore useful perhaps to give Oppen's later description of the meaning of the title & work:

> As in mathematics. A pure mathematical series would be one in which each term is derived from the preceding term by a rule. A discrete series is a series of terms each of which is empirically derived, each one of which is empirically true. And this is the reason for the fragmentary character of those poems. I was attempting to construct a meaning by empirical statements, by imagist statements.
>
> (Interview in *Contemporary Literature*, Spring 1969)

Oppen's later work has so far appeared in *The Materials* (1962), *This in Which* (1965), *Of Being Numerous* (1968); & Fulcrum Press in England printed *The Complete Poems* in 1972.

The small nouns
Crying faith
In this in which the wild deer
Startle, and stare out

DISCRETE SERIES
1929–1933

We have ceased, I think, to believe that a
nation's literature is anyone's personal property

EZRA POUND

The knowledge not of sorrow, you were
   saying, but of boredom
Is — aside from reading speaking
   smoking —
Of what, Maude Blessingbourne it was,
   wished to know when, having risen,
' approached the window as if to see
   what really was going on ' ;
And saw rain falling, in the distance
   more slowly,
The road clear from her past the window-
   glass —
Of the world, weather-swept, with which
   one shares the century.

I

White. From the
Under arm of T

The red globe.

Up
Down. Round
Shiny fixed
Alternatives

From the quiet

Stone floor . . .

2

      Thus
Hides the

Parts—the prudery
Of Frigidaire, of
Soda-jerking —

Thus

Above the

Plane of lunch, of wives
Removes itself
(As soda-jerking from
the private act

Of
Cracking eggs);

big-Business

The evening, water in a glass
Thru which our car runs on a higher road.

Over what has the air frozen ?

Nothing can equal in polish and obscured
      origin that dark instrument
A car
      (Which.
Ease; the hand on the sword-hilt

Her ankles are watches
(Her arm-pits are causeways for water)

When she steps
She walks on a sphere

Walks on the carpet, dressing.
Brushing her hair

Her movement accustomed, abstracted,
Declares this morning a woman's
' My hair, scalp — '

1

The three wide
Funnels raked aft, and the masts slanted

                    the
Deck-hand slung in a bosun's chair
Works on this 20th century chic and
                    efficiency
Not evident at ' The Sailor's Rest '.
2

The lights, paving —
This important device
Of a race

Remains till morning.

                    Burns
Against the wall.
He has chosen a place
With the usual considerations,
Without stating them.
Buildings.

The mast
Inaudibly soars; bole-like, tapering :
Sail flattens from it beneath the wind.
The limp water holds the boat's round
                    sides. Sun
Slants dry lights on the deck.
                    Beneath us glide
Rocks, sand, and unrimmed holes.

Closed car — closed in glass —
At the curb,
Unapplied and empty :
A thing among others

Over which clouds pass and the
                    alteration of lighting,
An overstatement
Hardly an exterior.
Moving in traffic
This thing is less strange —
Tho the face, still within it,
Between glasses — place, over which
                    time passes — a false light.

Who comes is occupied
Toward the chest (in the crowd moving
            opposite
Grasp of me)
                    In firm overalls
The middle-aged man sliding
Levers in the steam-shovel cab, —
Lift (running cable) and swung, back
Remotely respond to the gesture before last
Of his arms fingers continually —
Turned with the cab. But if I (how goes
                    it?) —
                    The asphalt edge
Loose on the plateau,
Horse's classic height cartless
See electric flash of streetcar,
The fall is falling from electric burst.

PARTY ON SHIPBOARD

Wave in the round of the port-hole
Springs, passing, — arm waved,
Shrieks, unbalanced by the motion —
Like the sea incapable of contact
Save in incidents (the sea is not
      water)
Homogeneously automatic — a green capped
      white is momentarily a half mile
      out —
The shallow surface of the sea, this,

Numerously — the first drinks —
The sea is a constant weight
In its bed. They pass, however, the sea
Freely tumultuous.

This land :
The hills, round under straw ;
A house

With rigid trees

And flaunts
A family laundry,
And the glass of windows

Semaphoring chorus,
The width of the stage. The usher from it :
Seats' curving rows two sides by distant
        phosphor. And those ' filled ';
Man and wife, removing gloves
Or overcoat. Still faces already lunar.

The edge of the ocean,
The shore : here
Somebody's lawn,
By the water.

She lies, hip high,
On a flat bed
While the after-
Sun passes.

Plant, I breathe —
                O Clearly,
Eyes legs arms hands fingers,
Simple legs in silk.

Civil war photo :
Grass near the lens;
Man in the field
In silk hat. Daylight.

The cannon of that day
In our parks.

As I saw
There
Year ago——
If there's a bird
On the cobbles ;
One I've not seen

———————————————————

Bolt
In the frame
Of the building——
A ship
Grounds
Her immense keel
Chips
A stone
Under fifteen feet
Of harbor
Water——
The fiber of this tree
Is live wood
Running into the
Branches and leaves
In the air.

———————————————————

From this distance thinking toward you,
Time is recession

Movement of no import
Not encountering you

Save the pulse cumulates a past
And your pulse separate doubly.

———————————————————

Town, a town,
But location
Over which the sun as it comes to it;
Which cools, houses and lamp-posts,
        during the night, with the roads——

Inhabited partly by those
Who have been born here,
Houses built—. From a train one sees
     him in the morning, his morning;
Him in the afternoon, straightening——
People everywhere, time and the work
     pauseless :
One moves between reading and re-reading,
The shape is a moment.
From a crowd a white powdered face,
Eyes and mouth making three——
Awaited—locally—a date.

Near your eyes —
Love at the pelvis
Reaches the generic, gratuitous
        (Your eyes like snail-tracks)

Parallel emotions,
We slide in separate hard grooves
Bowstrings to bent loins,
       Self moving
Moon, mid-air.

Fragonard,
Your spiral women
By a fountain

' 1732 '

Your picture lasts thru us

      its air
Thick with succession of civilizations;
And the women.

No interval of manner
Your body in the sun.
You ? A solid, this that the dress
       insisted,

Your face unaccented, your mouth a mouth ?
                    Practical knees :
It is you who truly
Excel the vegetable,
The fitting of grasses — more bare than
                              that.
Pointedly bent, your elbow on a car-edge
Incognito as summer
Among mechanics.

' O city ladies '
Your coats wrapped,
Your hips a possession

Your shoes arched
Your walk is sharp

Your breasts
            Pertain to lingerie

The fields are road-sides,
Rooms outlast you.

Bad times :
The cars pass
By the elevated posts
And the movie sign.
A man sells post-cards.

It brightens up into the branches
And against the same buildings

A morning :
His job is as regular.

On the water, solid —
The singleness of a toy —

A tug with two barges.

O what O what will

Bring us back to
Shore,
        the shore

Coiling a rope on the steel deck

DRAWING

Not by growth
        But the
Paper, turned, contains
This entire volume

Deaths everywhere —
The world too short for trend is land —
        In the mouths,
        Rims

In this place, two geraniums
In your window-box
Are his life's eyes.

Written structure,
Shape of art,
More formal
Than a field would be
(existing in it) —
Her pleasure's
Looser ;
' O — '

        ' Tomorrow ? ' —

Successive
Happenings
(the telephone)

Note. The rules above have been inserted for purposes of space here to
mark long spaces, or discreet pagination between poems in earlier versions
of the "Series."—J.R.

Kenneth Patchen

Born 1911 in Niles, Ohio. Died 1972. He lived for many years in California & participated, in spite of a long-term spinal illness, in both the San Francisco Renaissance & poetry-jazz readings with the Chamber Jazz Sextet & others. But the character of his work was formed in the 1930s & through it he was the major transmitter in his person of the role of poet-prophet. First identified as a "proletarian poet," he began to shape a vision of "love" in the context of a threatening politics: a theme & voice that would be reawakened in many by the Vietnam experience of the 1960s. At the same time he experimented with new visions & forms: surreal narratives & landscapes, visual poetry, illuminated (often hand-painted) books, & apocalyptic poem-novels, that explored the seer's role from a number of directions, *in* & *out* of the poem. His books to the mid–40s included *Before the Brave* (1936), *First Will & Testament* (1939), *Teeth of the Lion* (1942), *The Dark Kingdom* (1942), *Cloth of the Tempest* (1943), *Outlaw of the Lowest Planet* (1946), *Panels for the Walls of Heaven* (1947); & the currently available gatherings are *Collected Poems* (New Directions, 1969) & *Poems of Humor & Protest* (City Lights, 1960).

Have you wondered why all the windows in heaven were broken?
Have you seen the homeless in the open grave of God's hand?
Do you want to acquaint the larks with the fatuous music of war?

"LET US HAVE MADNESS OPENLY"
Let us have madness openly, O men

Of my generation. Let us follow
The footsteps of this slaughtered age:
See it trail across Time's dim land
Into the closed house of eternity
With the noise that dying has,
With the face that dead things wear—
                    nor ever say

We wanted more; we looked to find
An open door, an utter deed of love,
Transforming day's evil darkness;
                but
We found extended hell and fog
Upon the earth, and within the head
A rotting bog of lean huge graves.

AS SHE WAS THUS ALONE IN THE CLEAR MOONLIGHT,
standing between rock and sky, and scarcely seeming to touch
the earth, her dark locks and loose garments scattered by the
wind, she looked like some giant spirit of the older time, prepar-
ing to ascend into the mighty cloud which singly hung from
this poor heaven

so when she lay beside me
sleep's town went round her
and wondering children pressed against the high windows
of the room where we had been

so when she lay beside me
a voice, reminded of an old fashion:
            "What are they saying?
            of the planets and the turtles?
            of the woodsman and the bee?"
but we were too proud to answer, too tired to care about designs
            "of tents and books and swords and birds"

thus does the circle pull upon itself
and all the gadding angels draw us in

until I can join her in that soft town where the bells
split apples on their tongues
and bring sleep down like a fish's shadow.

CONTINUATION OF THE LANDSCAPE

Definite motion is accomplished
Where all seems fixed in the orderly molds
Of sight (through the mastery and knowledge
        of natural signs we can renew
        ourselves with an ancient innocence):
These forests have the sanctity of the quiet tides
Rolling over their green reaching, yet
They do not improve upon their real station,
Which is to grow as it was first decreed.
The white bird and the snail vary the world
By the exact condition of their being; only man
Would change his distance from that beautiful center;
Only man, undirected and naked, would run
From the creature which inhabits his kind.

That to this dark village, unsummoned, unattended
By guide or acclaim, with more joy than sorrow,
I come; is not without its moment on the clock
Of my endeavor. Only through losing our place
        in this overlapping circle of wombs,
        can we attain to that ultimate pattern
Where childhood selects its running wing and grave.

*

A queen with transparent breasts is found
On the slope of the black hill.
She has a flowing and a meaning
Which the distance dims.
Shape of head distorted by three long swinging poles
That seem to batter through her skull—

Though this may be no more than the lances
Of her companions, who are obscured
By the way the air is torn across in that place.
In fact, this whole scene is frayed and indistinct,
Almost as if it had been too long in the world,
And seen by no one really to make it luminous.

A man made of water and a shoulder-high heart
Are proceeding at a slow pace before.
Just behind come two pretty scintillating claws
Dressed as tavern maids, one of them
Riding on the horns of a small yellow wolf.
They are all intent on an object or ideal
Which seems to be harbored just above me.
The heart moves its head from side to side,
And in each of its eyes there is a tiny slit
Through which a cross looks.

THE EDUCATION OF THE WATERS

THE GRAND PALACE OF VERSAILLES

An elephant made of cotton . . .
Towers of lace under which satin-heeled
Gentlemen sit, playing with the bustles
Of slightly desiccated Grandes Damns.
Good morning, Louis; it's a fine day
In the mirror.

A chaise longue carved
Out of the living body of a white leopard . . .
Spools of silk placed in buckets
Of gilt milk . . . A three-headed dancer
Prancing to the music of a little bell
Languidly swung by a Negro with a hairlip.
Two visiting kings having their canes reheaded,
While a painter to the court tints their eyebrows
With the juice of mildly sickening berries.
What does Salvador Ernst Matta, Louis?
It's a fine day in the mirror.

From PANELS FOR THE WALLS OF HEAVEN

Bloodspout lamp milkgreenmilk they never asked me so I never told them when you come to the green druss turn shrilly and run like hell it won't help the game's no good any look you weigh it Big Juicy Kill I think the reason is the power is without any glory whatever is . green . a . color . green . or . an . object . like . a smile is is enough to get you through the day is coming right down to it your idea of fun is doing it the hard way going to help keep your marbles in place is settling your bull in fill your kind of people is it getting about time to put a few things of some purity together so that any dreer or bobling spin or felthy nane or chaivened spoke green thigh wrist ounce of shame green Green Is The Thought Of The Sea Bones clattering on a grin of sind respect for things comes first I've been awake at night seeing the way people suffer without any hope that the foot will ever lift off their necks it isn't right that human beings should be eaten alive. City. Lark. Finger. Kind men die. The grass breast is without nourishment. The dry paws of words who me honey go on go on say it tell them I'm hiding in here oh I should never have come to bed with you you and your Aristotle technique certainly mam if it isn't a good book we've got it paws of words picking the noses of dead men. Lampspout blood The leetle men are getting scairt of their world. Charlie Hearse is hobbling your way and the promised awa

THE NATURE OF REALITY

Bed.   Apple.

  Sly bird.   Policeman.

    Famine.   Rod of milk.

      Dice.   Groan.

        Stone.   Towel.

          Divot.

"Put some on mine."   Six or Tad Prichard.

THE REALITY OF NATURE

                    Seeking

            death   life

        growth   decay

      peace   madness

    conflict   silence

  birth   dissolution

"Put some in me."   Tad Prichard or none.

T E R R O R E

grocer have you any Hethnid pears

ALL THESE OF US ARE DOOMED

they have a delightful sunny taste

The Thought Of

"I ALWAYS RETURN TO THIS PLACE"

I always return to this place . . .

Roar and howl in the leaf! The astonished eye
Looking out of the air at me

O the astonished eye looking out of the air
At me—I always return to this place,
To this Gate, this Throne, this dread Altar—

I always return to the Mystery . . . *The astonished eye
Looking out of the air at me*

And I think there is nothing in the world but the Mystery

Kenneth Rexroth

Born 1905 in South Bend, Indiana. Early years in Chicago & New York City, later in California. An independent, self-educated poet, translator, man-of-letters, he was a younger & necessary counter to the line of Pound, offering alternative strategies for renewal, translation & assimilation of the past, calling attention to concerns that others had largely ignored or rejected: the full range of contemporary European & South American modernism, Amerindian & other tribal poetries, the work of overlooked contemporaries, & many of the new poets of the 1950s & 60s. He entered early into the avant garde enterprise, as a painter first, then as the proponent of a "cubist" approach to the poem (see below), & was, along with Zukofsky himself, the major younger contributor to Z.'s "*Objectivists*" *Anthology* (1932). (Possibly because of his rejection of Pound's centrality, he's almost never included among the "objectivist" poets.) His work also appeared in magazines like *Blues* & *Pagany*, but his first book, *In What Hour*, wasn't published until 1941 (the earlier cubist poems of *The Art of Worldly Wisdom* didn't appear until 1949), by which time the direction of his work was towards a "more accepted idiom," extensions (largely Eastern in origin) of lyricism, landscape & meditation, & the frequent use of a syllabic line. He was a contributor to Creeley's *Black Mountain Review* in the early 1950s, & his elegy for Dylan Thomas, "Thou Shalt Not Kill," while not typical of the later work, was an incentive to the public bardic style identified with the Beat poets of the middle 50s. During that time too he was a central figure in the San Francisco Renaissance & important participant in the poetry-jazz experiment. The major collections of his work are *The Complete Collected Shorter Poems* (including *The Art of Worldly*

Wisdom, In What Hour, & *The Phoenix & the Tortoise*) & *The Collected Longer Poems* (including *Prologomenon to a Theodicy* from 1925), along with translations from modern French & Spanish poetry, classical Chinese, Japanese, Greek, etc. His writings on poetry & society, etc. appear in books like *Bird in the Bush, Assays, The Alternative Soviety,* & *American Poetry in the 20th Century.*

Cubism in poetry . . . is the conscious, deliberate dissociation and recombination of elements into a new artistic entity made self-sufficient by its rigorous architecture.

When I was a young lad I thought that literary Cubism was the future of American poetry. Only Walter Conrad Arensberg in his last poems, Gertrude Stein in Tender Buttons *and a very few other pieces, much of the work of the young Yvor Winters and others of his generation of Chicago Modernists, Laura Riding's best work and my own poems later collected in* The Art of Worldly Wisdom *could be said to show the deliberate practice of the principles of creative construction which guided Juan Gris or Pierre Reverdy. . . . In verse such as Reverdy's . . . the primary data of the poetic construction . . . are simple, sensory, emotional or primary informative objects capable of little or no further reduction. Eliot works in* The Waste Land *with fragmented and recombined arguments; Pierre Reverdy with dismembered propositions from which subject, operator and object have been wrenched free and restructured into an invisible or subliminal discourse which owes its cogency to its own strict, complex and secret logic.*

Poetry such as this attempts not just a new syntax of the word. Its revolution is aimed at the syntax of the mind itself. Its restructuring of experience is purposive, not dreamlike, and hence it possesses an uncanniness fundamentally different in kind from the most haunted utterance of the Surrealist or Symbolist unconscious.

FUNDAMENTAL DISAGREEMENT
WITH TWO CONTEMPORARIES

for Tristan Tzara & André Breton

1

> "From any event intervals radiate in
> all directions to other events, and the
> real and imaginary intervals are sepa-
> rated by a cone which is called the
> null-cone."
>   gonaV

   ;

ing   ev

          IT

  dras   pRoG

           2m3nL$\frac{1}{2}$

         pros

  *proS

instoting

tismaD

PROXY

gela

  domi

    immoderate

PROSPECT

savours curve doing instant conceptual bipartite

        engine

West inclination 32

PERSPECTIVE

engine

ENGINE

MACHINE

CONCEPTUAL PERSPECTIVE ENGINE

  x y z

motor-organ-organ-motor-.....................ds!

number here

$\sqrt{2}$ to the left   to the right

distribute

origin of vector
description of vectors
the personal pronoun
vvvvvvvvvvv
  vvvvvvvvv
    vvvvvvv
              v
i
modulatepersistendurereverserevolvereciprocate-
  oscillateperpetuate
ARRIVE
or pressure of significance
there exists an a
there exists an i
there exists at least one other entity b
valid
efficient
potent
which vests the prospect with originative continuity
the dominative pervasive accomodation of aspect
as the insertion localized as integer formaliter
thus acquiring trajectory
thus assimilating contingency
or the contingent as hiatus in the populous
meaning fused with recipient
amplitude coexists with discretion
importance endures with intervals
concentric and unique
not pendant
as an exterior
without contour
without projective meaning
shift digit
for this the fundamental number
of momentum
of retrograde traction
or of ingress
incarnate

tenuous
fluent
for this ophidian throat
twilight under the eucalyptus
stones sabers clouds kings nights leaves wishes
   arbors sparks shells wings mouths stars oranges
   fabrics ewes queens skins vehicles accents seeds
   cinders chutneys mixtures fevers apes eggs
   corpses mosses boxes shades irons glaciers
go up as if to be in or on
contemplate acumen distinguished as a formation
or the inane as mother of density
where the embassy of acquisition scrutinizes the
      monitor
or the spoon out of the sessile rainbow slides to the
    left of the mountains we are so prone to leave
    out of our calculations

   2

"The sea cucumber when in danger of being eaten, eviscerates itself,
shooting out its soft internal organs as a sop to the enemy while the
body wall escapes and is able to regenerate a new set of viscera."

a

Profoundly and in state as casualty
the confusion lowered in
the reversible cross, the lowered
white cross thrust, glass baubled
integer in foam embroidery,
visual pollen seething between
the lashes, each focussed tendon
sown with eye bloom, each crowded
lily laminated with voracious
mouths. Ominous
the distinct difference. Lethal
the cleft intention. The flesh
motor in fog. The carnivorous

fungus of unpictured scene.
The gifts: a little cloud
a soiled handkerchief crumpled in a ball
the rose in alcohol
the brussels sprout in a sabot.
Electric and furry, that thing
hides in some worn
anonymous viscera, and now
summer being ended, the clocks
bulge, the liquescent
bulbs drop from the boughs, and splash
pale in the starlight on the stone.
That is your ambush, your gift, for your heels
will slide in the dark, your frosted onion
crash, its myriad capsules explode
ordure over the environs.

b

Now the hammock sword ensnares the febrile tree
palms ungloving haste across the sky
bloom veils off the wooly cormorant and race
of eye against returning
spears. So slice recurring
value, the spinner slicing
the red sphere concurs in taps
grounds soon and offers
which scattered crow or a blue sphere.
Revealing neither the arteries
of a fist nor peeling the iliac fascia.
A green bar
indifferent to imposition
reluctant as cruciform
cold as laminated, discovers
the horse wedge hammered
in crepuscular wind, or toss-pebbles
at night, late.
It was delievered in chunks and piled all over

at the end there was a termite left alone at the top
Should the honey comb
tossed from the rail of the liner
sink slowly
down
beyond the reach of the sun's rays
lower than life
which is impossible.

c

Glitter ghost
flame death as rose blossom
the poinsettia smashed in night.
Once late between the graves
the dogs sitting in a circle
waiting in the grey sand
o narthex, narthex
the crescents broken everywhere.
The chinaman in the dawn hurried
north between the mountains.
The second day, before light, the dome
flamed, the boy
spoke of the sea
and something ancient in a white casket.
Then appeared
like a seal through a paper hoop
the scarlet egg of the lunation
roaring through the sky
uprooting the brass trees
passing noiselessly
over the deserted cities
over the ghosts in nickel shrouds
over the moss green and purple headlands
over the grey sea.
The children approach the hyena diffidently
they approach the guardian of embers
the sky filled with red hands

the wind heavy with dry salt
o narthex
broken on the walls

d

As from the citron kelp untangling in the purple bay
only brain caryatids return
hands jewelled with seeds
only the red dog circles the rocks
so from the ivory cautiously the spatulate question
intrudes, mutters itself, branches in the room of souls.
So the oak leaves, whittled in copper
parade death and astonishment
so, carefully as an animal in a dream, blue
with an icy pelvis
unaware of secrets, the chronometer
bursts, first crimson, in the triangle
of Leo, then orange
in the belt of Orion.
The grey larvae of the oak leaves
spill voluminously out of the proscenium.
Mackerel hang in the waterspout.
And eyelids are shorn like foreskins
in this religion
and the wand is weighted with eyeballs
and the ice cream skull weeps
that never should have stayed
that will never leave.

e

How shall the stars on the cheeks
of this mandrill find a number.
They have seen stars as intervals.
They have broken the vermilion legs of the jungle.
They wait
the owl

the moth
the tower in flames
the ibis with multiple moist paps.
None other waits.
The cross gouged in the hummock
waits like a trap.
Over the white trees the stars
iris out in the sky
metallic breaths cross the air
and distinct against the dry grass
the black bears
the red baboons
wait, and the little girl
so pale, so fragile waited
naked, whispering to herself.
In the ravines the pilgrims foundered in the mire
their jaws were broken, they died
and lay unburied.

INTO THE SHANDY WESTERNESS
for William Carlos Williams

Do you understand the managing.
Mornings like scissors
Leaves of dying.
Let even particle e. Point track m-n.
Cooling grey slender ascenders.
Congruence. Yes? that's what you thought it would be?
A flag waves, a kite climbs. Clouds climb, advancing impalpable
    edges.
The whole mottled sky turns slowly on its zenith, the same clouds
    go round and round the horizon.

As A is.
A triangular chessboard squared in two tones of grey, P to K3,
    KN x B.
It's very cold under the table. A cold window.
When he was little he used to go out to the barn and put his cheek

against a cow and cry and cry. When he swam in the pasture
creek the little fish tickled his legs.

Something is going to cut.

Something is going to break.

I don't see it I can't hear it but it's swinging.

One goes swiftly back. One goes forward. Two move to the left.
A voice.

The steel column bores and bores into the ground. Presently the air
is filled with ammonia fumes.

We will sing hymn number 366, "Art thou weary, art thou languid,"
366

MY number, MY bleeding number. So I ups and tells em Why I was
weary Why I was languid.

As B is.

Orange green yellow blue red violet.

Is there anybody there said the stranger. Is there any reason why
after all these difficulties we should be subjected in this par-
ticular humiliating manner.

Orange. Row after row of shining minute faces. Green. A slight
lurch and then the floor begins to climb smoothly steadily up
up everything clatters against the altar. The celebrant is em-
barrassed. White discs fly from the cylindrical heads of the
spectators and disappear out of the windows. Presently only
their palpitating necks are left, hollow, dark purple inside.

It's pleasant to think of the cottages along the mountainside. The
alfalfa ripening in the afternoon. The thin smoke of evening.
The chill nights.

Assorted solutions, neat packages of peace were distributed by
officious archangels. There was much unemployment, long
breadlines everywhere in the dusty cities, quiet, no traffic, much
patience. We came on, collecting visas, wasting our substance
in bribes, asking, Who is king in this kingdom, who is your
ruler, by what do you measure?

Whenever I think of England I see Wyndham Lewis standing in a
high freezing wind on the plain where Mordred and Arthur
fought, dressed only in his BVD's painfully extracting thorns
from his chapped buttocks. It grows dark rapidly.

When I think of France I see Marcel Duchamp on Michigan Boulevard in a raccoon coat and a number of young americans praying before a roller-coaster from which middle-aged frenchmen strapped to bicycles leap into tubs of cocacola.

Now the blue flowers return the gravel mornings.
Now the immaculate mistresses
And those we loved from afar.
It's yellow in the sunlight and blue around the corner and it's all been so simple. The grey furry plants and the white hands. The considerations, the ablatives. The conversation about death. The lace parasol.
He was naturally very neat.
He was particular about neckties and very proud of his razors. They gleamed on maroon plush. His watch lost sixty seconds every four weeks neither more nor less. He sat on the screen porch smelling faintly of citronella and spoke slowly and distinctly of love. Then he died. And she hadn't made up her mind. So she walked under the lace parasol avoiding the decayed catalpa blossoms that littered the sidewalk.

It grows dark. A shitepoke flies up from the canal. That's a shitepoke he says to the boy. For supper hassenpfeffer. The rabbits are getting at the tomato sets, bad. Tourists are camping down at the woodlot at the corner. You can see their fire from the back door. When they came for water Nero snapped at the man. Now he looks over at their fire and barks every few minutes. On both sides of the walk about every ten feet all the way to the gate bushel baskets are turned upside down over the peonies. As it gets darker they disappear.

EASY LESSONS IN GEOPHAGY
(for Hart Crane and Harry Crosby)

"*pulldo pulldo shows quoth the caliver*"—EASTWARD HOE

I

The Leonids having fallen
The tinkles having fallen

The silver having fallen silently
Having the fog
Having the colorless margin
Having the gold bees
The act having been forgotten
The right hand having turned sinister
Can the indifferent arms be raised
Moving in the tree tops
Sounding the long horn
Seeing the red animals
Floating among the transparent medusae
Canopus hears the moon hears
The night the members
Of the body move in the sea
In the saline transparent sea
Auguries of struggle urge the somatic
Community fluent webs run
Through the viscera the head
Appears in air the nostrils
The eyes open the lips open the whites
Of the eyes shine over
The groundswell the great conch speaks
The knowledge of war spreads over the water
The brittle bones watching
The spider
In a bar of light
In the sound of water

2

"In time all haggard hawks will stoop to lure"
The needle digests the eagle
The tile eyeballs
The painted marbles
The falsetto tornado interrupts itself
With shaved foxhounds
With unworthy insights
With hand-painted paraboloids
With cotton metronomes

With little beetles
The needle digests the eagle
They have programs in going
Away went conquests
Away went nodes and interruptions
Away went unmistakable punctuations
The kite screams and falls screaming
And falls blood streaming from its eyes
And falls its beak shattered
And falls in a tangent to the horizon
And falls whirling
And falls in mixed helices
And falls screaming
And falls into the spinning freezer
The resilient thumb presses the patent mattress
Three glimmers replace the hair
The scalp moves in recurrent conchoids
The undulation digests the albatross
Little cubes
The base whistle continues
Endures like the green hippocephali
Endures like the acknowledged error
Endures like the Gulf of Spoiled Botanies
Endures like the mincer
Endures like the worms of longitude
Ostriches digest needles
The dead are fed to the vultures
And the broken rhythmic vertigo recurs continually

3

"Born into it
Proved by external effects
Proved by internal effects
Thus literally living in a blaze of reality"
Is it fear to meet as he might meet fear
Meeting himself in the burnt forest
Is it fear avoiding the personal

Pronoun avoiding the eponymoi of myself
Amongst the innumerable black infusoria
I come so to the comet traps
I come so to the gegenschein
I come so to the more obscure aurora
I come so to the vital organs
Arranged on a shelf above the body
Guarded by the effigies of their patrons
When they spoke of a man they said you see
That was a different time in another
Place they spoke of another they said instead
Of succulents do you prefer kelp
Or cactus instead
Of the calipers the splintered ice

4

I passed the black fountain
I passed the swathed man
I passed the meteorite
I passed the tireless mice
I passed the long shark of the dawn
I passed the multitude of gelid eardrums
There are no teeth in most orchids
The bas-relief tilts in the wall
Flowers explode beneath the feet of the horses
And the earthquake announces its genesis by whistling in the ther-
        mometers, and
Announces its approach by obscuring the pulsations of the flowers
The earthquake speaks gently and distinctly in a foreign language.

Born into it
Proved by external effects
Proved by internal effects
Light is reddened by age, it loses energy as it gets older, traveling
        through space.

Charles Reznikoff

Born 1894 in Brooklyn. A decade older than the other "objectivists" (Oppen, Rakosi, Zukofsky), he developed from Pound's "imagisme" an approach intensely of his own world: "Jewish, American, urban," but set down with clear lines "pithy & plain" enough to transform a single perception into a poem. Later he would contrast his way to the "symbolist" idea that "to name is to destroy—to suggest is to create," asserting

> To name and to name and to name—and to name in such a way that you have rhythm, since music . . . is also part of the meaning.

A lawyer by profession, his strategy as a poet was to view the poetic act as itself a kind of testimony, the burden strongly on the seen & heard. His first book, *Poems*, appeared in 1920, followed by *Five Groups of Verse* (self-published, 1927), three Objectivist Press books, *Jerusalem the Golden* (1934), *In Memoriam: 1933* (1934) & *Separate Way* (1936), *Going to & Fro & Walking Up & Down* (1941), & *Inscription 1944–56* (1959). His "selected poems," *By the Waters of Manhattan,* is currently available, along with *Testimony: The United States 1885–1890,* a kind of found poetry derived from the language of court records, "to locate," Robert Creeley wrote, "the given instance sans direction, in the intense particularity of time and place." His sense of time & place ("Jewish, American, urban") emerges too in his novel, *By the Waters of Manhattan* (1930), & *Family Chronicle* (1963).

From **FIVE GROUPS OF VERSE (1927)**

1

THE IDIOT

With green stagnant eyes,
arms and legs
loose ends of string in a wind,

keep smiling at your father.

2

EPIDEMIC

Streamers of crepe idling before doors.

3

TWILIGHT

No stars
in the blue curve
of the heavens,
no wind.

Far off,
a white horse
in the green gloom
of the meadow.

4

GHETTO FUNERAL

Followed by his lodge, shabby men stumbling over the cobblestones,
and his children, faces red and ugly with tears, eyes and eyelids
    red,
in the black coffin in the black hearse the old man.

No longer secretly grieving
that his children are not strong enough to go the way he wanted
    to go
and was not strong enough.

CHARLES REZNIKOFF · 213

5

The ceaseless weaving of the uneven water.

6

From the fog a gull flies lowly
and is lost in fog. The buildings are only clouds.

7

How difficult for me is Hebrew:
even the Hebrew for *mother*, for *bread*, for *sun*
is foreign. How far have I been exiled, Zion.

THE SOCIALISTS OF VIENNA*
The rain is falling
steadily. Two by two,
a column of policemen marches
in the twilight. (Revolution!
Against our boots
strike,
flickering tongues!)
A company of soldiers
with machine-guns,
squad by squad, turns within a square
and marches down a street. (Revolution!
We are the greyhounds—
unleash us!—
to hunt these rabbits
out of the fields. *Listen to me,
my two wives,
I have killed a man!*)
Workingmen troop down the stairs

* I am indebted to Ilya Ehrenbourg's *Civil War in Austria* (*New Masses*,
July 3, 1934) for information.

and out into the rain;
hurrah!
Revolution! (The gentleness of the deer
will never persuade the tiger from his leap.
Strong as a million hands,
what Bastille or Kremlin withstands us
as we march, as we march?)

Who minds the rain now?
How bright the air is;
how warm to be alive!
No children
in the hallways;
the stores closed,
not a motor car;
except for the rain,
how quiet.

Revolution!
Hurry to the power-house;
let the water out of the
boilers! The wires of the lamps burn dimly,
the lights in the houses
are out. Tie the red flag to the chimney,
but do not go through the streets,
where the steel-helmets have woven nets
of barbed wire;
bring guns and machine-guns
through the sewer
to each beleaguered house;
and send couriers throughout the land,
Arise, arise, you workers!
Revolution!

Put on your helmets;
troopers, tighten the straps
under your chins;
strap on revolvers;
tighten your belts,

and mount your horses; mount!
Send bullets flying
through the panes of glass—
windows, mirrors, pictures;
forward, trot!
I am Fey,
I am Prince Starhemberg;
behind me is The Empire—
the princes of Austria
and the captains of Germany,
armored tanks and armored aeroplanes,
fortresses and battleships;
before us only workingmen
unused to arms and glory!

The bones in his neck part as they hang him,
and the neck is elongated;
here is a new animal
for the zoo in which are
mermaid, centaur, sphynx, and Assyrian cherub—
the face human, like their faces,
but sorrowing for a multitude,
hands and feet dangling
out of sleeves and trousers become too short,
and the neck a giraffe's—
as the neck of one who looks away from the patch of grass at
    his feet
and feeds among clouds should be.

Tell of it you who sit in the little cafés,
drinking coffee and eating whipped cream
among the firecrackers of witticisms;
tell of it you who are free to gallop about on horseback
or to ride in automobiles, or walk in gardens,
who say, Do not speak of despondency—
or any ugliness;
"Wie herrlich leuchtet
Mir die Natur!

Wie glaenzt die Sonne,
Wie lacht die Flur!"*

Karl Marx Hof, Engels Hof,
Liebknecht Hof, Matteotti Hof—
names cut in stone to ornament a house
as much as carving of leaves or fruit,
as any bust of saint and hero;
names pealing out a holiday among the ticking of clocks!—
speak your winged words, cannon;
shell with lies, radios,
the pleasant homes—
the houses built about courtyards
in which were
the noise of trees and of fountains,
the silence of statues and of flowers;
cry out, you fascists,
Athens must perish!
Long live Sparta!

AUTOBIOGRAPHY: HOLLYWOOD

I

I like the streets of New York City, where I was born,
better than these streets of palms.
No doubt, my father liked his village in Ukrainia
better than the streets of New York City;
and my grandfather the city and its synagogue,
where he once read aloud the holy books,
better than the village
in which he dickered in the market-place.
I do not know this fog,
this sun, this soil, this desert;
but the starling that at home

* How splendidly Nature is alight before me! How the sun is shining, how
the meadows laugh!—Goethe.

skips about the lawns
how jauntily it rides a palm leaf here!

II

I like this secret walking
in the fog;
unseen, unheard,
among the bushes
thick with drops;
the solid path invisible
a rod away—
and only the narrow present is alive.

III

I like this walk in the morning
among flowers and trees.
Only the birds are noisy.
But if they talk to me,
no matter how witty or wrong,
I do not have to answer;
and if they order me about,
I do not have to obey.

IV

These plants
which once halted the traveller
with thick thorny leaves
and clusters of spines
have become ornaments
to guard beds of flowers.

V

In the picture,
a turbaned man and a woman are seated in a garden
in which—this very tree
with large white blossoms like tulips.
It is a long way from Persia to the Pacific,
and a long time from the Middle Ages;
yet both picture and blossoming tree
have lived through time and tide.

VI

A clear morning
and another—yet another;
a meadow bright with dew;
blue hills
rising from a lake of mist;
single flowers
bright against a whitewashed wall
and scattered
in the grass;
flowers in broad beds
beside the narrow walk;
look, soldiers of Ulysses,
your spears
have begun to flower, too!

VII

I look at the opaque red of the passion-flower coldly
and at these bright odorless flowers
that grow so closely. The poppies are still most beautiful
(that grew in the fields before any gardener)
through whose yellow translucent petals
the sun shines
as they stand straight on the slender stems,
native to the soil and sun—
a bright democracy, a company yet each alone.

VIII

The bush beneath my window has grown
until now a twig
is reaching over the sill
as if to show
its cluster of delicate leaves.
You are beautiful, leaves, and silent:
you ask nothing—
neither food nor a fee
nor even that I look at you.

CHARLES REZNIKOFF · 219

IX   RAINY SEASON

It has been raining for three days.
The faces of the giants
on the billboards
still smile,
but the gilt has been washed from the sky:
we see the iron world.

X

The cold wind and black fog and the noise of the sea.

XI

The paths are deserted as always;
below, lights of houses and motor cars
and the broad wash of foam;
here, under the stars, beds of flowers, gloom of thick hedges,
and the orderly clusters of palm leaves.
If this were in Italy, you say,
the walks would be crowded.
And here would be rows of tables—
a band would be playing.
Is silence too strong for you?
Must it be diluted
with alcohol, conversation, and music?

XII

The Greeks would have made a myth about you, my fine girl,
and said a god, because of this indifference,
because you walk away quickly, turning
your beautiful head with its sleek black hair away,
changed you into the starling that flies with angry cries
from branch to branch
after the indifferent passer-by.

XIII

The flies are
flying about

and about
the middle of the room—
jerkily
in geometrical figures:
what are they trying to prove—
my guardian angels?

I have said good morning to the man at the door,
good morning to the man polishing the stairs.
Seated in my armchair,
on a cushion,
I, the shepherd, stare at my flock—
ten flies.
I came penniless
and found only a few,
never bothered my head about them,
did not pay them,
neither gave them to eat or to drink
nor even spoke to them,
and, look!
I shall cross the Jordan with at least twelve flies,
maybe, twelve times twelve:
how unworthy am I
of all this generosity!

I have become poor, it seems:
my flies are gone—except one
flying jerkily
about the room.
You do not buzz, my fly:
deep in thought, no doubt.
That is well.
I, too, am learning how to be silent,
and have learnt long ago how to be alone.

Laura Riding

Born 1901 in New York City, now publishes as Laura (Riding) Jackson. A poet who, in her own words, "identified poetic and human seriousness in a poetry intensely personal, yet not individualistic," she ascribes all this to an underlying "dedication to linguistic integrity," which, she tells us, was what brought about her eventual "renunciation of poetry." This came soon after publication of her *Collected Poems* (1938), when she found poetic seriousness "irremediably compromised ... by its subjecting linguistic integrities to aesthetic requirements, as if there were no resultant linguistic loss." She aimed then at "clarifying a mode of word-use ... more serious humanly and intrinsically than the ordinary, that needed, yet, no aesthetique for successful impact of word, success in it being a pure success of language."

Early in her life as a poet she had gone abroad to live. "In that English and cross-Atlantic literary atmosphere, there was, instead of crowding individualism [i.e., as in America], a loose assemblage of unsure positions, occupied with a varying show of modernistic daring; I had there a solitariness in which to probe the reality of poetry as a spiritual, not merely literary, inheritance." As the "center" of all her other writing (criticism, stories, a novel, etc.), "poetry seemed where the verbal maximum could be one with and the same as the truth maximum. When ... after pressing the linguistic possibilities of poetic utterance to further and further limits, I comprehended that poetry had no provision in it for ultimate practical attainment of that rightness of word that *is* truth ... I *stopped*." (*Contemporary Poets of the English Language*, 1971) She then concentrated her attention on language, "its intrinsic provisions"— or what she calls "the organic veracities of word-meaning"—& on what might be achieved "in 'trueness of word,' beyond the qualified truth-potential of poetry, or any other literarily verbal style."

Besides the major gathering of her poetry (*Collected Poems*, 1938), a selection, arranged & prefaced by her, appeared recently as *Selected Poems: In Five Sets* (Faber & Faber, 1970; Norton, 1973). Among her other works were a number of books of criticism, three of them collaborations, including *A Survey of Modernist Poetry* (second author: Robert Graves). As editor of *Epilogue* (four volumes, 1935–1938), she introduced "new critical orientations"— fostering in this, & as partner in the Seizin Press, the work of other writers. Later she worked (with her husband, Schuyler B. Jackson, d. 1968) on a book on language, which she is now completing; published articles; & brought out what she considers her most important published work to date, *The Telling* (Harper & Row, 1973), designed to be "a pronouncement both intimate and humanly comprehensive on the nature of personal being, and the speaking function." Though most of her earlier work is now out of print, her poetry, like her criticism, has exerted—& still exerts—a substantial, often unacknowledged influence. "My poetic work," she says, "has been as a private workshop resource to poets, with scant regard for its intrinsic nature and title to public credit as of intrinsic importance."

*"I have written that which I believe breaks the spell of poetry"**

BY CRUDE ROTATION
By crude rotation—
It might be as a water-wheel
Is stumbled and the blindfolded ox
Makes forward freshly with each step
Upon the close habitual path—
To my lot fell a blindness

* From Preface to *Selected Poems* (1970)—presumable reference to use of words in *The Telling*.

That was but a blindedness,
And then an inexpressive heart,
And next a want I did not know of what
Through blindedness and inexpressiveness
Of heart.

To my lot fell
By trust, false signs, fresh starts,
A slow speed and a heavy reason,
A visibility of blindedness—these thoughts—
And then content, the language of the mind
That knows no way to stop.

Thus turning, the tragedy of selfhood
And self-haunting smooths with turning,
While the worn track records
Another, and one more.

To my lot fell
Such waste and profit,
By crude rotation
Too little, too much,
Vain repetition,
The picture over-like,
Illusion of well-being,
Base lust and tenderness of self.
Fall down, poor beast,
Of poor content.
Fly, wheel, be singular
That in the name of nature
This creaking round spins out.

ELEGY IN A SPIDER'S WEB

What to say when the spider
Say when the spider what
When the spider the spider what

The spider does what
Does does dies does it not
Not live and then not
Legs legs then none
When the spider does dies
Death spider death
Or not the spider or
What to say when
To say always
Death always
The dying of always
Or alive or dead
What to say when I
When I or the spider
No I and I what
Does what does dies
No when the spider dies
Death spider death
Death always I
Death before always
Death after always
Dead or alive
Now and always
What to say always
Now and always
What to say now
Now when the spider
What does the spider
The spider what dies
Dies when then when
Then always death always
The dying of always
Always now I
What to say when I
When I what
When I say
When the spider
When I always

Death always
When death what
Death I says say
Dead spider no matter
How thorough death
Dear or alive
No matter death
How thorough I
What to say when
When who when the spider
When life when space
The dying of oh pity
Poor how thorough dies
No matter reality
Death always
What to say
When who
Death always
When death when the spider
When I who I
What to say when
Now before after always
When then the spider what
Say what when now
Legs legs then none
When the spider
Death spider death
The genii who cannot cease to know
What to say when the spider
When I say
When I or the spider
Dead or alive the dying of
Who cannot cease to know
Who death who I
The spider who when
What to say when
Who cannot cease
Who cannot

Cannot cease
Cease
Cannot
The spider
Death
I
We
The genii
To know
What to say when the
Who cannot
When the spider what
Does what does dies
Death spider death
Who cannot
Death cease death
To know say what
Or not the spider
Or if I say
Or if I do not say
Who cannot cease to know
Who know the genii
Who say the I
Who they we cannot
Death cease death
To know say I
Oh pity poor pretty
How thorough life love
No matter space spider
How horrid reality
What to say when
What when
Who cannot
How cease
The knowing of always
Who these this space
Before after here
Life now my face

The face love the
The legs real when
What time death always
What to say then
What time the spider

THE WIND, THE CLOCK, THE WE

The wind has at last got into the clock —
Every minute for itself.
There's no more sixty,
There's no more twelve,
It's as late as it's early.

The rain has washed out the numbers.
The trees don't care what happens.
Time has become a landscape
Of suicidal leaves and stoic branches —
Unpainted as fast as painted.

Or perhaps that's too much to say,
With the clock devouring itself
And the minutes given leave to die.

The sea's no picture at all.
To sea, then: that's time now,
And every mortal heart's a sailor
Sworn to vengeance on the wind,
To hurl life back into the thin teeth
Out of which first it whistled,
An idiotic defiance of it knew not what
Screeching round the studying clock.

Now there's neither ticking nor blowing.
The ship has gone down with its men,
The sea with the ship, the wind with the sea.
The wind at last got into the clock,

The clock at last got into the wind,
The world at last got out of itself.

At last we can make sense, you and I,
You lone survivors on paper,
The wind's boldness and the clock's care
Become a voiceless language,
And I the story hushed in it —
Is more to say of me?
Do I say more than self-choked falsity
Can repeat word for word after me,
The script not altered by a breath
Of perhaps meaning otherwise?

POET: A LYING WORD

You have now come with me, I have now come with you, to the season that should be winter, and is not: we have not come back.

We have not come back: we have not come round: we have not moved. I have taken you, you have taken me, to the next and next span, and the last—and it is the last. Stand against me then and stare well through me then. It is a wall not to be scaled and left behind like the old seasons, like the poets who were the seasons.

Stand against me then and stare well through me then. I am no poet as you have span by span leapt the high words to the next depth and season, the next season always, the last always, and the next. I am a true wall: you may but stare me through.

It is a false wall, a poet: it is a lying word. It is a wall that closes and does not.

This is no wall that closes and does not. It is a wall to see into, it is no other season's height. Beyond it lies no depth and height of further travel, no partial courses. Stand against me then and stare well through me then. Like wall of poet here I rise, but am no poet as walls have risen between next and next and made false end to leap. A last, true wall am I: you may but stare me through.

And the tale is no more of the going: no more a poet's tale of a going false-like to a seeing. The tale is of a seeing true-like to a knowing: there's but to stare the wall through now, well through.

It is not a wall, it is not a poet. It is not a lying wall, it is not a lying word. It is a written edge of time. Step not across, for then into my mouth, my eyes, you fall. Come close, stare me well through, speak as you see. But, oh, infatuated drove of lives, step not across now. Into my mouth, my eyes, shall you thus fall, and be yourselves no more.

Into my mouth, my eyes, I say, I say. I am no poet like transitory wall to lead you on into such slow terrain of time as measured out your single span to broken turns of season once and once again. I lead you not. You have now come with me, I have now come with you, to your last turn and season: thus could I come with you, thus only.

I say, I say, I am, it is, such wall, such poet, such not lying, such not leading into. Await the sight, and look well through, know by such standing still that next comes none of you.

Comes what? Comes this even I, even this not-I, this not lying season when death holds the year at steady count—this every-year.

Would you not see, not know, not mark the count? What would you then? Why have you come here then? To leap a wall that is no wall, and a true wall? To step across into my eyes and mouth not yours? To cry me down like wall or poet as often your way led past down-falling height that seemed?

I say, I say, I am, it is: such wall, such end of graded travel. And if you will not hark, come tumbling then upon me, into my eyes, my mouth, and be the backward utterance of yourselves expiring angrily through instant seasons that played you time-false.

My eyes, my mouth, my hovering hands, my intransmutable head: wherein my eyes, my mouth, my hands, my head, my body-self, are not such mortal simulacrum as everlong you builded against very-death, to keep you everlong in boasted death-course, never-long? I say, I say, I am not builded of you so.

This body-self, this wall, this poet-like address, is that last barrier long shied of in your elliptic changes: out of your leaping, shying, season-quibbling, have I made it, is it made. And if now poet-like it rings with one-more-time as if, this is the mounted stupor of your everlong outbiding worn prompt and lyric, poet-like—the forbidden one-more-time worn time-like.

Does it seem I ring, I sing, I rhyme, I poet-wit? Shame on me then! Grin me your foulest humour then of poet-piety, your eyes rolled up in white hypocrisy—should I be one sprite more of your versed fame—or turned from me into your historied brain, where the lines read more actual. Shame on me then!

And haste unto us both, my shame is yours. How long I seem to beckon like a wall beyond which stretches longer length of fleshsome traverse: it is your lie of flesh and my flesh-seeming stand of words. Haste then unto us both. I say, I say. This wall reads 'Stop!' This poet verses 'Poet: a lying word!'

Shall the wall then not crumble, as to walls is given? Have I not said: 'Stare me well through'? It is indeed a wall, crumble it shall. It is a wall of walls, stare it well through: the reading gentles near, the name of death passes with the season that it was not.

Death is a very wall. The going over walls, against walls, is a dying and a learning. Death is a knowing-death. Known death is truth sighted at the halt. The name of death passes. The mouth that moves with death forgets the word.

And the first page is the last of death. And haste unto us both, lest the wall seem to crumble not, to lead mock-onward. And the first page reads: 'Haste unto us both!' And the first page reads: 'Slowly, it is the first page only.'

Slowly, it is the page before the first page only, there is no haste. The page before the first page tells of death, haste, slowness: how truth falls true now at the turn of page, at time of telling. Truth one by one falls true. And the first page reads, the page which is the page before the first page only: 'This once-upon-a-time when seasons failed, and time stared through the wall nor made to leap across, is the hour, the season, seasons, year and years, no wall and wall, where when and when the classic lie dissolves and nakedly time salted is with truth's sweet flood nor yet to mix with, but be salted tidal-sweet—O sacramental ultimate by which shall time be old-renewed nor yet another season move.' I say, I say.

From MEMORIES OF MORTALITIES
[1] *My Mother and My Birth*

My mother was a snake, but warm:
In her a welling heart, spite unfrozen.
Hating, she loved.
Coiling to choke, she kissed.

And men were done then
Slowing in same doom-pause,
Same morrow of old sun.
They were about their deaths then—
They were worn, then, men,
To scant remainders of themselves,
And their kinds were fatal
As comes the flowering-day
When seedlings take their names
And are the final things—
Which in their labelled promise
Seemed the first giant garden
Where beauty is such tropic horror
That death to make fright's suddenness
And self-sensation is not needful.

It being then such lateness
Of world, death-season,
Flowering, name-taking,
The cold snake to its melting came—
She was Contempt of Time,
That Spirit which at Origin
Bittered against the taste false-sweet
Of Future, on her lightning tongue
Already poison and corrupted Past.
This was my mother,
Who, when the mortal lag took haste
And death became contemporary,
Turned fond, and loved the flesh despised—
As ghouls the living love,
Their griefs claiming, adoring their disease.

Hers was the paradox I chose
To have heretic body of:
I, Spirit which at End
Greets remnant Now, to make
Beginning, in this prompt decline,
Of death's all-soon respited day,
Which, dawning infinite from death
Like night from night, encompasses
Entirety in its utter light:
This Self of Subsequence
To Time personally structured,
Touched, touching, minded, minding,
Interbreathing, interbreathed:
I, smalled laterness than Time,
My double-tongued snake-mother's singler meaning.

And it was idiot nature,
There to be babe, outfrowning from unborn,
And there to suckle swooning,
Giddy with dreadful newness of myself,
Clutching the stranger-breast
As shipwrecked orphan chooses
One stranger from the rest for friend,
By logic of confusion and by need
Of privacy against the many.

So fallible that nature:
For, being, I was none of her,
And she, delivered of me, held
No backward life of mine.
That union in material magic—
Her larger-than-herself; untrue extreme,
With my so smaller-than-self leastness—
Had magic's aftermath,
Materiality's division:
As if it had not been,
And she to snakehood's tears again,

And I to opposite sense of death—
Who yet an early flesh could have
Because Contempt of Time, relenting
On Time's sickness of time,
Grew time-like, stayed death's full succession.
For, in this mock-beneficence,
Regret, aged Nothingness, took change
And was dissolving Everything—
By whose sophistry of flesh with spirit
Twilight-same, I argued me a body,
A flesh-prelude to myself,
With ancestry in snake-slough cast
Like silence from loud dumbness.

Oh, obscure!
Birth, body, is by darkness,
And mine by that opacity
Which, being death's late dawn,
Looms mystery-bright at truth-verge.
This night-time that I wage,
My temporal person, prophet of myself
In lazy mouth's futurities,
Must live, precede me mortally,
That I inherit of myself
By refutation of those semblances
Which liker, liker, are less like
To ultimate me as I remember
Oh, how not-like all to this survival
Of myself, this very-me made last
Of strange approximation to myself
In eager hesitancies—
Lest quickness of me be too instant,
And I but the unproven echo
Of dispersed original.

Therefore such quickness as makes life,
The stuttering slow grammaring of self

That death with memoried seeming crowns.
And were I otherwise myself
Than in a near-mistaken mask's
Gradual fading into true-face,
Then were I no fit face to welcome
Gradual Now familiarly to death,
No visible pied voice to mingle
Natural with garish hearing,
No idiom of life-translation
Leading Time to after-dwelling,
No almost-lie to warrant truth by,
No long event of me by which
To contradict eventfulness—
Oh, Contradiction,
World-being, human condition,
Stolen grace, outrage unfinal:
What farthest Next is End,
Composure, whole Cessation?
Nearer and nearer Next, till Now,
The measure over-fine, impossible,
Contradiction's life-length
Cut to the moment which is life and death
In one unlivable solution.
Then comes pure death, the grace compelled,
Duration cleansed of day-change.

In such rhythm of nearness, nextness, nowness,
From present arrestation borne a motion
Motionless toward present progress,
Thus I in fellowed dying walked
To Subsequence—taking the numerous path
That Time had greatly narrowed to,
Arriving there as at a home
General to all who dare be so undone,
Save for mortality remembered.

NOTHING SO FAR

Nothing so far but moonlight
Where the mind is;
Nothing in that place, this hold,
To hold;
Only their faceless shadows to announce
Perhaps they come —
Nor even do they know
Whereto they cast them.

Yet here, all that remains
When each has been the universe:
No universe, but each, or nothing.
Here is the future swell curved round
To all that was.

What were we, then,
Before the being of ourselves began?
Nothing so far but strangeness
Where the moments of the mind return.
Nearly, the place was lost
In that we went to stranger places.

Nothing so far but nearly
The long familiar pang
Of never having gone;
And words below a whisper which
If tended as the graves of live men should be
May bring their names and faces home.

It makes a loving promise to itself,
Womanly, that there
More presences are promised
Than by the difficult light appear.
Nothing appears but moonlight's morning —
By which to count were as to strew
The look of day with last night's rid of moths.

STATEMENT OF DISAGREEMENTS (January 1974).* Because Mrs. Jackson takes strong exception to the implications of the title of this book, and disagrees with certain editorial views of which she is aware, she has been invited to record her objections and differing views. She rejects, for instance, the idea that there is anything in common between the hard questioning she pursues in her later work and attitudes to poetry found currently among poets. She regards these as generally "using poetry to give literary legitimacy to positions that are but variations on stock modernistic sophistication, which lack even the pretentions of earlier modernistic poetry to bases of intellectually respectable poetic theory." She regards as dangrous misinterpretation the idea that the characterization of her poetic work (presented in the preface of her *Selected Poems*) as going beyond the poetic as a literary category, and reaching into the field of the general human ideal of speaking, can have any relevance to possibilities now in *poetic* practice: the idea transmutes her renunciation of poetry as—even to the point to which she was able to take it—linguistically defective into medicine for poetry, she declares. She further rejects the idea that as poet she did any redefining of poetry, was as a poet a revolutionary in respect to poetry. "It was my thorough fidelity to the historic propositions of poetry as to the union in it of creed of right word and craft of sensuous phoneticalities that enabled me to discover how creed gets trimmed by craft." She denies the editorial thesis that there has been in the 20th century any questioning of the very nature and value of poetry ("the dissidents, the rebels, have held on tight to the literary perquisites of poet-identity"), and denies that her poetic work, and her later thinking and work, are historically related to any poetic movement of the century. "What I did as a poet was a unique trial. In what I did next, in what I did after, I knew no other laborer in the same field, in my time, except one. No practising poet could have kinship with me in that."

As to "Revolution of the Word": she would be dissociated both from "revolution" in this phrase, which she views as transmogrified from a political term, itself a derivative from the general word, into a sentimental carry-all of implications of literary or poetic radicalism. And she would be dissociated from "The Word" of the phrase, "as implying linguistic radicalism serving literary radicalism, and suggesting a mythologically sacred extra-linguistic entity, property of a religion of poetry." Before her renunciation of poetry, she committed herself, she says, "to both the propieties of language and to the proprieties of poetry as being perfectly harmonious." After the renunciation, "my sense of the importance of *words* (always literally real to me, never conceived of through a totemic obstraction 'Word') increased in solemnity. *They*, as *language*, I know as the sufficient apparatus, of themselves, without interventions of art, for the personal acts of truth that all human beings owe their expressive natures, and one another, and the cosmic reality that bred them. What is wanting is a new loyalty to the values of language, inhering in words

---

* The "statement" is given exactly as written by Laura Riding Jackson.

in the distinctions they effect: these are the values of truth as the active principle and quality of reason. A turning again to relearn their words is the common need of human beings, now. Such a conception as a 'Revolution of the Word' takes the human linguistic condition into new degrees of ignorance of words' meaning-substance—not into new poetic enlightenment, but into deeper shades of irrationality than those into which general linguistic habitudes have been descending."

[Note: After writing the above on REVOLUTION OF THE WORD, I learned, very late, that the subtitle A NEW GATHERING OF AMERICAN AVANT GARDE POETRY 1914–1945 was to follow that phrase. I feel keenly uncomfortable under that title, but because of time and space emergencies I rest at a brief comment: I reject the term "avant-garde" as having no historical or critical applicability to my poetic work. I disapprove of it as being, with its context of European literary politicism, not generally applicable to American poetry of the period in question, and otherwise only very narrowly applicable, if at all, and if so to certain elements of it at its earlier and later worst.

L.R.J.]

Louis Zukofsky

Born 1904 in New York City. "Specifically, a writer of music," he quotes in a "prose" section of *29 Songs*, & that concern is everywhere in his work, which seems now more innovative of forms & the hidden resources of language's soundings than that of any but a handful of American moderns. But the music, if the term holds, is as much of eyes as ear, the consequence of "the kind of intelligence Zukofsky has—seeing & hearing words in the world as the specific possibilities they contain" (R. Creeley). First published in Pound's *Exile* (later in *Dial, Blues, Pagany, Criterion*, etc.), he coined the word "objectivists" (his quotes), to fit an issue of younger poets he was assembling for *Poetry* (1931); later extending it to *An "Objectivists" Anthology* (1932) & to George & Mary Oppen's To Publishers, renamed The Objectivist Press. Not a polarization into object/subject but a dialectic, the objectivist "principle" derives from a metaphor of vision ("rays of the objective brought to a focus," as in optics) & from earlier assumptions (mainly Pound's) about image & vortex. Thus, to catch Zukofsky in quotes about it then & later:

    (1) "thinking with the things as they exist"

or (2) "(as) Shakespeare's text thruout favors the clear physical eye against the erring brain"

or (3) "the direction of historic & contemporary particulars."

The major collections of Zukofsky's work are *All: The Collected Short Poems 1923–58* & *All* (ditto) *1956–1964*, & two large works, *A* (a long "poem of a life," begun in 1927, most of the projected 24 "movements" now in print) & *Bottom: On Shakespeare* (in prose, "a long poem on a theme for the variety of its recurrences"). His translations from Catullus (1969)—starting from the sound & moving out—break new ground for translation-as-composition & are, like his musical *Autobiography* (1970), a collaboration with his wife, Celia. His writings on poetry, aside from the above, are in *Prepositions: Collected Critical Essays* (1968) & *A Test of Poetry* (1964).

The melody, the rest are accessory—
. . . my one voice; my other . . .
An objective—rays of the object brought to a focus,
An objective—nature as creator—desire for what is objectively
perfect,
Inextricably the direction of historic and contemporary particulars.

TWO SONGS

        It's a gay li - ife
There's naw - - - thing
        lak po - - - ee try
it's a delicacy
        for   a horse:

Dere's na - - - thing
        lak pea-   nut-brittle
it's a delicacy
        for   the molars.

·

            No One Inn

P.S.   i.e.   almost dreamt
the face against the door
a pastel's   a boy's

who owns it   being in a war
plays the market early
hires a chef   would look at his chef's hat

flour not at the exchange of
the exchanges   the margin drops
gets the chef walking   and preparing

it a cork   please,
be it, whose thought is it
floated   and by a house-boat

if there   wound 's sleep, to be sure
" then bacteria in mercurochrome ? " — yes
if you want peroxide I will give you — thrive

the windings   an inn
the windings   a face in an inn
the windings   no one is in in No One Inn

From POEM BEGINNING "THE"
FIFTH MOVEMENT: *Autobiography*

186   Speaking about epics, mother,
187   How long ago is it since you gathered
                mushrooms
188   Gathered mushrooms while you mayed.
189   It is your mate, my father, boating
190   A stove burns like a full moon in a desert night.
191   Un in hoyze is kalt. You think of a new
                grave,
192   In the fields, flowers.
193   Night on the bladed grass, bayonets dewed.
194   It is your mate, my father, boating.
195   Speaking about epics, mother,—

196 Down here among the gastanks, ruts,
        cemetery-tenements—
197 It is your Russia that is free.
198 And I here, can I say only—
199   "So then an egoist can never embrace
        a party
200   Or take up with a party?
201   Oh, yes, only he cannot let himself
202   Be embraced or taken up by the party."
203 It is your Russia that is free, mother.
204 Tell me, mother.

205 Winged wild geese, where lies the passage,
206 In far away lands lies the passage.
207 Winged wild geese, who knows the pathway?
208 Of the winds, asking, we shall say:
209 Wind of the South and wind of the North
210 Where has our sun gone forth?
211 Naked, twisted, scraggly branches,
212 And dark, gray patches through the branches,
213 Ducks with puffed-up, fluttering feathers
214 On a cobalt stream.
215 And faded grass that's slowly swaying.
216 A barefoot shepherd boy
217 Striding in the mire:
218 Swishing indifferently a peeled branch
219 On jaded sheep.
220 An old horse strewn with yellow leaves
221 By the edge of the meadow
222 Draws weakly with humid nostrils
223 The moisture of the clouds.
224 Horses that pass through inappreciable
        woodland,
225 Leaves in their manes tangled, mist, autumn
        green,
226 Lord, why not give these bright brutes—
        your good land—
227 Turf for their feet always, years for their mien.

228 See how each peer lifts his head, others follow,
229 Mate paired with mate, flanks coming full
              they crowd,
230 Reared in your sun, Lord, escaping each hollow
231 Where life-struck we stand, utter their praise
              aloud.
232 Very much Chance, Lord, as when you first made us,
233 You might forget them, Lord, preferring what
234 Being less lovely where sadly we fuss?
235 Weed out these horses as tho they were not?
236 Never alive in brute delicate trembling
237 Song to your sun, against autumn assembling.

238 If horses could but sing Bach, mother,—
239 Remember how I wished it once—
240 Now I kiss you who could never sing Bach,
              never read Shakespeare.
241 In Manhattan here the Chinamen are yellow
              in the face, mother,
242 Up and down, up and down our streets they
              go yellow in the face,
243 And why is it the representatives of your,
              my, race are always hankering for
              food, mother?
244 We, on the other hand, eat so little.
245 Dawn't you think Trawtsky rawthaw a
              darrling,
246 I ask our immigrant cousin querulously.
247 Naw! I think hay is awlmawst a Tchekoff.
248 But she has more color in her cheeks than
              the Angles—Angels—mother,—
249 They have enough, though. We should
              get some more color, mother.
250 If I am like them in the rest, I should
              resemble them in that, mother,
251 Assimilation is not hard,
252 And once the Faith's askew

253   I might as well look Shagetz just as much
                 as Jew.
254   I'll read their Donne as mine,
255   And leopard in their spots
256   I'll do what says their Coleridge,
257   Twist red hot pokers into knots.
258   The villainy they teach me I will execute
259   And it shall go hard with them,
260   For I'll better the instruction,
261   Having learned, so to speak, in their
                 colleges.
262   It is engendered in the eyes
263   With gazing fed, and fancy dies
264   In the cradle where it lies
265   In the cradle where it lies
266   I, Senora, am the Son of the Respected
                 Rabbi,
267   Israel of Saragossa,
268   Not that the Rabbis give a damn,
269   Keine Kadish wird man sagen.

SONG 22: "TO MY WASH-STAND"

        To my wash-stand
in which I wash
        my left hand
and my right hand

        To my wash-stand
whose base is Greek
        whose shaft
is marble and is fluted

        To my wash-stand
whose wash-bowl
        is an oval
in a square

      To my wash-stand
whose square is marble
         and inscribes two
smaller ovals to left and right for soap

      Comes a song of
water from the right faucet and the left
         my left and my
right hand mixing hot and cold

      Come a flow which
if I have called a song
         is a song
entirely in my head

       a song out of imagining
modillions descried above
         my head   a frieze
of stone completing what no longer

      is my wash-stand
since its marble has completed
         my getting up each morning
my washing before going to bed

      my look into a mirror
to glimpse half an oval
         as if its half
were half-oval in my head   and the

      climates of many
inscriptions human heads shapes'
         horses' elephants' (tusks) others'
scratched in marble tile

      so my wash-stand
in one particular breaking of the
         tile at which I have
looked and looked

        has opposed to my head
the inscription of a head
        whose coinage is the
coinage of the poor

        observant in waiting
in their getting up mornings
        and in their waiting
going to bed

        carefully attentive
to what they have
        and to what they do not
                have

when a flow of water
        doubled in narrow folds
occasions invertible counterpoints
        over a head   and

        an age in a wash-stand
and in their own heads

"MANTIS"

Mantis! praying mantis! since your wings' leaves
And your terrified eyes, pins, bright, black and poor
Beg—"Look, take it up" (thoughts' torsion)! "save it!"
I who can't bear to look, cannot touch,—You—
You can—but no one sees you steadying lost
In the cars' drafts on the lit subway stone.

Praying mantis, what wind-up brought you, stone
On which you sometimes prop, prey among leaves
(Is it love's food your raised stomach prays?), lost

Here, stone holds only seats on which the poor
Ride, who rising from the news may trample you—
The shops' crowds a jam with no flies in it.

Even the newsboy who now sees knows it
No use, papers make money, makes stone, stone,
Banks, "it is harmless," he says moving on—You?
Where will be put *you*? There are no safe leaves
To put you back in here, here's news! too poor
Like all the separate poor to save the lost.

Don't light on my chest, mantis! do—you're lost,
Let the poor laugh at my fright, then see it:
My shame and theirs, you whom old Europe's poor
Call spectre, strawberry, by turns; a stone—
You point—they say—you lead lost children—leaves
Close in the paths men leave, saved, safe with you.

Killed by thorns (once men), who now will save you
Mantis? what male love bring a fly, be lost
Within your mouth, prophetess, harmless to leaves
And hands, faked flower,—the myth is: dead, bones, it
Was assembled, apes wing in wind: On stone,
Mantis, you will die, touch, beg, of the poor.

Android, loving beggar, dive to the poor
As your love would even without head to you,
Graze like machined wheels, green, from off this stone
And preying on each terrified chest, lost
Say, I am old as the globe, the moon, it
Is my old shoe, yours, be free as the leaves.

Fly, mantis, on the poor, arise like leaves
The armies of the poor, strength: stone on stone
And build the new world in your eyes, Save it!

"MANTIS," AN INTERPRETATION

OR NOMINA SUNT CONSEQUENTIA RERUM,
NAMES ARE SEQUENT TO THE THINGS NAMED

Mantis! praying mantis! since your wings' leaves
      Incipit Vita Nova
      le parole . . .
      almena la loro sentenzia
the words . . .
at least their substance

at first were
"The mantis opened its body
It had been lost in the subway
It steadied against the drafts
It looked up—
Begging eyes—
It flew at my chest"

      —The ungainliness
      of the creature needs stating.

No one would be struck merely
By its ungainliness,
Having seen the thing happen.

Having seen the thing happen,
There would be no intention 'to write it up,'

But *all* that was happening,
The mantis itself only an incident, *compelling any writing*
The transitions were perforce omitted.

Thoughts'—two or three or five or
Six thoughts' reflection (pulse's witness) of what was happening
All immediate, not moved by any transition.

Feeling this, what should be the form
Which the ungainliness already suggested
Should take?

            —Description—lightly—ungainliness
            With a grace unrelated to its surroundings.

Grace there is perhaps
In the visual sense, not in the movement of
"eyes, pins, bright, black and poor."

Or considering more than the isolation
Of one wrenched line,

Consider:
"(thoughts' torsion)"
la battaglia delli diversi pensieri . . .
the battle of diverse thoughts—
The actual twisting
Of many and diverse thoughts

What form should *that* take?
            —The first words that came into mind
            "The mantis opened its body—"
            Which might deserve the trope:
            the feeling of the original which is a permanence

            ?

Or the feeling accompanying the first poor 27 words' inception
(the original which is a permanence
?),
That this thoughts' torsion
Is really a sestina
Carrying subconsciously
Many intellectual and sensual properties of the
            forgetting and remembering Head
One human's intuitive Head

                  Dante's rubric
                        Incipit
                  Surrealiste
                        Re-collection

A twisted shoe by a pen, an insect, lost,
"To the short day and the great sweep of shadow."

The sestina, then, the repeated end words
Of the lines' winding around themselves,
Since continuous in the Head, whatever has been read,
                    whatever is heard,
                        whatever is seen
Perhaps goes back cropping up again with
Inevitable recurrence again in the blood
Where the spaces of verse are not visual
But a movement,
With vision in the lines merely a movement.

What is most significant
Perhaps is that C—and S—and X—of the 19th century
Used the "form"—not the form but a Victorian
Stuffing like upholstery
For parlor polish,
And our time takes count against them
For their blindness and their (unintended?) cruel smugness.

Again: as an experiment, the sestina would be wicker-work—
As a force, one would lie to one's feelings not to use it

One feels in fact inevitably
About the coincidence of the mantis lost in the subway,
About the growing oppression of the poor—
Which is the situation most pertinent to us—,
With the fact of the sestina:
Which together fatally now crop up again
To twist themselves anew
To record not a sestina, post Dante,
Nor even a mantis.

Is the poem then, a sestina
Or not a sestina?

The word sestina has been
Taken out of the original title. It is no use (killing oneself?)

            —Our world will not stand it,
                the implications of a too regular form.

Hard to convince even one likely to show interest in the matter
That this regularity to which 'write it up' means not a damn

(Millet in a Dali canvas, Circe in E's Cantos)
Whatever seeming modelling after the event,
649 years, say, after Dante's first canzone,
If it came back immediately as the only
Form that will include the most pertinent subject of our day—
The poor—
Cannot mean merely implied comparison, unreality
Usually interpreted as falsity.

Too much time cannot be saved
Saying:
The mantis might have heaped up upon itself a
Grave of verse,
But the facts are not a symbol.

There is the difference between that
And a fact (the mantis in the subway)
And all the other facts the mantis sets going about it.

No human being wishes to become
An insect for the sake of a symbol.

But the mantis *can start*
History etc.
The mantis situation remains its situation,
Enough worth if the emotions can equate it,

"I think" of the mantis
"I think" of other things—
The quotes set repulsion
Into movement.

Repulsion—
Since one, present, won't touch the mantis,
Will even touch the poor—

but carefully.

The mantis, then,
Is a small incident of one's physical vision
Which is the poor's helplessness
The poor's separateness
Bringing self-disgust.

The mantis is less ungainly than that.

There should be to-day no use for a description of it
Only for a "movement" emphasizing its use, since it's been around,

An accident in the twisting
Of many and diverse "thoughts"
i.e. nerves, glandular facilities, electrical cranial charges
For example—
line 1—entomology
line 9—biology
lines 10 and 11—the even rhythm of riding under-
           ground, and the sudden jolt are also
           of these nerves, glandular facilities,
           brain's charges
line 12—pun, fact, banality
lines 13 to 18—the economics of the very poor—the
           newsboy—unable to think beyond
           "subsistence still permits competi-
           tion," banking, *The Wisconsin Elkhorn
           Independent*—"Rags make paper,
           paper makes money, money makes
           banks, banks make loans, loans make
           poverty, poverty makes rags."
lines 22 to 24—Provence myth
lines 25 to 29—Melanesian self-extinction myth
line 33—airships
lines 35 and 36—creation myth (Melanesia), residue of
           it in our emotions no matter if fetched
           from the moon, as against l. 25 to 29.
and naturally the coda which is the
only thing that can sum up the
jumble of order in the lines weaving

"thoughts," pulsations, running commentary, one upon the other,
itself a jumble of order
as far as poetic
sequence is concerned:

> the mantis
> the poor's strength
> the new world.

29—"in your eyes"
> the original shock still persisting—

So that the invoked collective
Does not subdue the senses' awareness,
The longing for touch to an idea, or
To a use function of the material:
The original emotion remaining,
    like the collective,
Unprompted, real, as propaganda.

The voice exhorting, trusting what one hears
Will exhort others, is the imposed sensuality of an age
When both propaganda and sensuality are necessary against—
"—we have been left with nothing
just a few little unimportant ships
and barges" (British Admiralty even in 1920)

or jelly for the Pope

la mia nemica, madonna la pieta
my enemy, my lady pity,

36—"like leaves"
The Head remembering these words exactly in the way it
> remembers

la calcina pietra
the calcined stone.

But it remembers even more constantly
the poor
than

com' huom pietra sott' erba
as one should hide a stone in grass.

Nor is the coincidence
Of the last four lines
Symbolism,
But the simultaneous,
The diaphanous, historical
In one head.

"A" 1

A
      Round of fiddles playing Bach.
          Come, ye daughters, share my anguish —
      Bare arms, black dresses,
          See Him! Whom?
      Bediamond the passion of our Lord,
          See Him! How?
His legs blue, tendons bleeding,
          O Lamb of God most holy!
Black full dress of the audience.
Dead century, where are your motley
Country people in Leipzig.
Easter,
Matronly flounces, starched, heaving,
Cheeks of the patrons of Leipzig —
"Going to Church? Where's the baby?"
"Ah, there's the Kapellmeister
      in a terrible hurry —
Johann Sebastian, twenty-two
      children!"

      The Passion According to Matthew,
      Composed seventeen twenty-nine,
      Rendered at Carnegie Hall,

Nineteen twenty-eight,
Thursday evening, the fifth of April.
The autos parked, honking.

A German lady there said:
   (*Heart turned to Thee*)
"I, too, was born in Arcadia."

The lights dim, and the brain when the flesh dims.
Hats picked up from under seats.
Galleries darkening.
"Not that exit, Sir!"
Ecdysis: the serpent coming out, molting,
As tho blood stained the floor as the foot stepped,
Bleeding chamfer for shoulder:
"Not that exit!"
"Devil! Which?" —
Blood and desire to graft what you desire,
But no heart left for boys' voices.
Desire longing for perfection.

And as one who under stars
Spits across the sand dunes, and the winds
Blow thru him, the spittle drowning worlds —
I lit a cigarette, and stepped free
Beyond the red light of the exit.

The usher faded thru "Camel" smoke;
The next person seen thru it,
Greasy, solicitous, eyes smiling minutes after,
A tramp's face,
Lips looking out of a beard
Hips looking out of ripped trousers
                              and suddenly
Nothing.
About me, the voices of those who had
                         been at the concert,
Feet stopping everywhere in the streets,
High necks turned for chatter:

"Poor Thomas Hardy he had to go so soon,
He admired so our recessional architecture —
What do you think of our new Sherry-Netherland!"
"Lovely soprano,
Is that her mother? lovely lines,
I admire her very much!"
And those who perused the score at the concert,
Patrons of poetry, business devotees of arts and letters,
                    Cornerstones of waste paper, —
"Such lyric weather" —
Chirping quatrain on quatrain;
And the sonneteers — when I consider
                    again and over again —
Immured holluschickies persisting thru polysyllables,
Mongers in mystic accretions;
The stealers of "mélange adultère de tout,"
Down East, Middle West, and West coast flaunters
                    of the Classics and of
                              Tradition
(A word to them of great contours) —
Who sang of women raped by horses.

And on one side street near an elevated,
Lamenting,
Foreheads wrinkled with injunctions:
"The Pennsylvania miners are again on the lockout,
We must send relief to the wives and children —
What's your next editorial about, Carat,
We need propaganda, the thing's
                    becoming a mass movement."

It was also Passover.

The blood's tide like the music.
A round of fiddles playing
Without effort —
As into the fields and forgetting to die.
The streets smoothed over as fields,
Not even the friction of wheels,

Feet off ground:
As beyond effort —
Music leaving no traces,
Not dying, and leaving no traces.

Not boiling to put pen to paper
Perhaps a few things to remember —

"There are different techniques,
Men write to be read, or spoken,
Or declaimed, or rhapsodized,
And quite differently to be sung";
"I heard him agonizing,
I saw him *inside*";
"Everything which
We really are and never quite live."
Far into (about three) in the morning,
The trainmen wide awake, calling
Station on station, under earth,

> *Cold stone above Thy head.*
> *Weary, broken bodies.*
> *Sleeping: their eyes were full of sleep.*

The next day the reverses
As if the music were only a taunt:
As if it had not kept, flower-cell, liveforever,
        before the eyes, perfecting.

— I thought that was finished:
Existence not even subsistence,
Worm eating the bark of the street tree,
Smoke sooting skyscraper chimneys,
That which looked for substitutes, tired,
Ready to give up the ghost in a cellar —
Remembering love in a taxi:
A country of state roads and automobiles,
But great numbers idle, shiftless, disguised on streets —

The excuse of the experts
'Production exceeds demand so we curtail employment';
And the Wobblies hollering reply,
Yeh, but why don't you give us more than a meal
        to increase the consumption!
And the great Magnus, before his confrères in Industry,
Swallow tail, eating a sandwich,
"Road map to the stomach," grinning,
Pointing to a chart, between bites.

"We ran 'em in chain gangs, down in the Argentine,
Executive's not the word, use *engineer*,
Single handed, ran 'em like soldiers,
Seventy-four yesterday, and could run 'em today,
Been fishin' all Easter
Nothin' like nature for hell-fire!"

Dogs cuddling to lamposts,
Maybe broken forged iron,
        " *Ye lightnings, ye thunders*
          In clouds are ye vanished?

        Open, O fierce flaming pit!"

#36

Strange to reach that age, re-member a

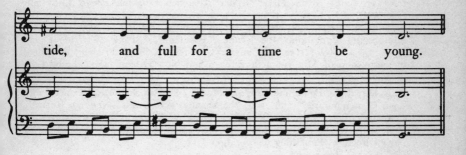

tide, and full for a time be young.

(continued from page vi)